Colorado
Rocky Mountain Country

Rand McNally Landmarks of America

Colorado
Rocky Mountain Country

Text and Photography
by Kent and Donna Dannen

RAND McNALLY & COMPANY
Chicago • New York • San Francisco

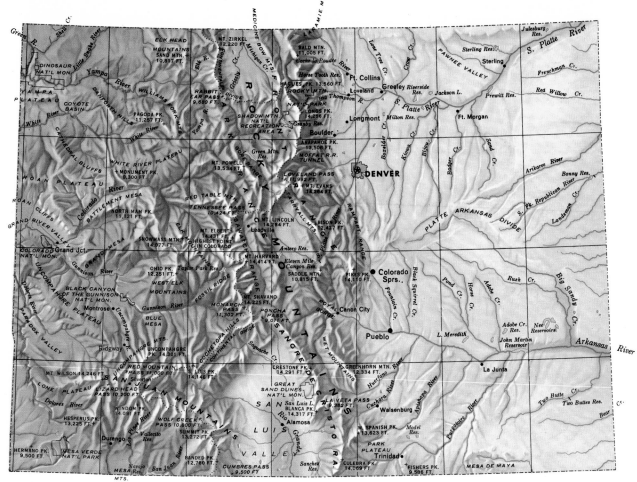

Map of Colorado

Overleaf: *Maroon Bells Wilderness and the Elk Mountains seen from McClure Pass, White River National Forest.*
Opposite page: *Quaking aspen leaves in autumn.*

Library of Congress Cataloging in Publication Data

Dannen, Kent, 1946–
　Colorado: Rocky Mountain country.

　(Rand McNally landmarks of America)
　1. Colorado—Description and travel. 2. Colorado—History. I. Dannen, Donna, 1949–　　. II. Title.
III. Series.
F776.D24　1983　　978.8　　83-8612
ISBN 0-528-81121-5

Printed in the United States of America
by Rand McNally & Company

First printing, 1983

Contents

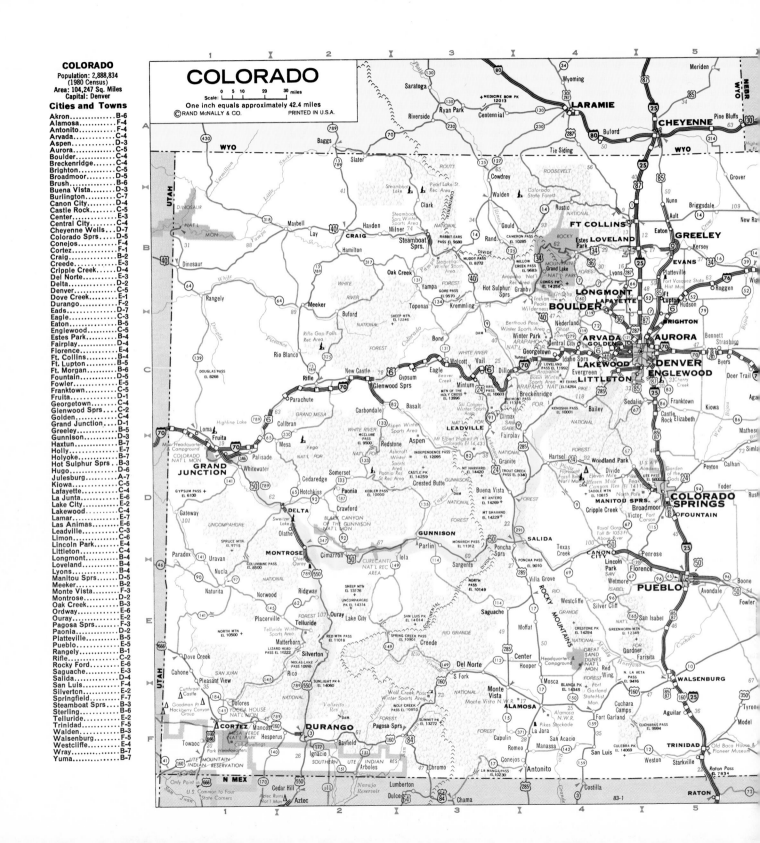

COLORADO

Population: 2,888,834
(1980 Census)
Area: 104,247 Sq. Miles
Capital: Denver

Cities and Towns

Rocky Mountain columbine is the state flower.

State of Surprise

Colorado is celebrated and explained in a profusion of books, articles, photographs, poems, maps, and songs. Even so, the state contains a seemingly infinite capacity to surprise both residents and visitors with its glorious variety. Beginning with the Indians and extending through European explorers, fur traders, miners, farmers, cowboys, and tourists, surprise has become a Colorado tradition.

The obviously artificial boundaries of the state account for some of Colorado's multiformity. In 1861, perfectly straight lines forming a rectangle were slapped down on a land of extreme diversity by Civil War–distracted congressmen who never had seen the place and knew little about it. Within Colorado, Sahara-like desert contrasts with lush forest and swampy meadow. Barren rock on mountain summits contrasts with deep and rich soil in river valleys. Nearly unbearable heat contrasts with perpetual snowbanks. And all of this can be experienced easily within a single day.

The state's rectangular outline belies its more complex and interesting shapes. The natural divisions of Colorado—plains in the east, high mountains in the middle, desertlike plateaus on the western edge—are easier to perceive when seeing them from an airliner. During a flight from Denver to Salt Lake City, for instance, Colorado unrolls as a colorful and detailed map beneath the wings of the plane. Increased speed and altitude compress perceptions of time and space. A view from on high clarifies concepts gained on the ground about the rising of mountains, dropping of valleys, excavation by glaciers, and erosion by rivers.

From Denver's Stapleton International Airport, airliners circle over plains covered with outwash debris from the eroding Front Range. This major range within the Rockies "fronts" onto the plains from near the Wyoming border south to Colorado Springs. Easily visible at the base of this range are sedimentary rocks, like those enclosing the acoustically excellent natural amphitheater of Denver's Red Rocks Park. Formed in the late Paleozoic period, about 300 million years ago, colorful slabs lie against the Front Range in various spots north and south to the end of sight. East of the red rocks are sharp, curved ridges of younger sedimentary rocks, known as hogbacks.

Approximately 70 million years ago, the continent of North America, as it drifted away from Europe, buckled along a zone of structural weakness that happens to run down the middle of Colorado. Thus began the rise of the Rockies, which today extend 3,000 miles from northern Alberta and British Columbia to southern New Mexico. The buckling of igneous and metamorphic rocks from deep beneath the surface upended horizontal sedimentary layers. The rubble of sedimentary rock that once lay on top of the mountains was washed onto the plains, leaving only tilted red slabs and hogbacks along the bases of high, snowcapped ranges.

Today's high peaks are formed primarily of rocks as old as 1,000 million to 1,750 million years, dredged by nature's forces from the continent's core. Prominent in the Front Range are Longs Peak, Mount Evans, and Pikes Peak—all "Fourteeners," peaks with summits over 14,000 feet above sea level. The hard rocks of incomprehensible age are riddled with fractures, weak zones where erosion occurs less slowly than on unyielding solid chunks of rock.

As the mountains began to rise, moisture eroded these fractures in many ways. Rushing water attacked the mountains. Trickling water penetrated cracks, alternately freezing and thawing, wedging off bits of rock as the ice expanded and contracted. Working slowly but invincibly, these forces had roughed out the present shape of the Rockies by about 3 million years ago.

Then came the glaciers to sculpt the finishing touches. More snow accumulated in winter near the

Iron-tinted rock formed from ancient mud flats rises 14,156 feet on the glaciated Maroon Bells above Maroon Lake. Brittle rock has killed climbers on the "Deadly Bells."

This page: *Glaciers sculpted all sides of Longs Peak, tallest in Rocky Mountain National Park. This view is from the popular cross-country ski trail to Dream Lake.*

Opposite page: *The east face of Longs Peak, a glacial headwall, towers 2,495 feet above a hiker enjoying dawn's warm light at Chasm Lake, dug out by the glacier 100 feet deep in the cirque's floor.*

tops of mountains than melted in summer. After 100 feet or more of packed snow and ice accumulated, the ice underneath all this weight became flexible and began to flow downhill. Glaciers were born.

As glaciers slowly flowed like rivers of ice from their points of origin, the headwalls, winter snows accumulating at the top replenished the ice. Ice formed at the tops of glaciers flowed down V-shaped valleys already carved by water erosion, broadening the valley floors to a U shape. When the ice touched the valley walls and

and scraping of peak and valley walls. Mountains that had glaciers on all sides were eaten away until the tops of glaciers merged, and the peaks were islands of rock surrounded by ice. Today these are cliff-sided towers, such as Longs Peak. In other areas, broad ridges remained above the ice line. A fascinating ecosystem of tiny, ground-hugging plants, the alpine tundra, can be found on these unglaciated summits.

At least three times glaciers flowed down Colorado mountain valleys, with the ice melting away during warm periods. The current warm period began about 10,000 years ago. Some scientists think that the earth is now enjoying a few thousand years of warmth before the glaciers again creep down from their headwalls to grind away everything in their paths and carve more gigantic sculpture on the face of the Rockies.

In northern Colorado, a few tiny glaciers remain from a miniglacial period about 300 years ago, which reached its height in the 1870s. The southernmost is Arapaho Glacier, on the flank of Indian Peaks Wilderness. This glacier is owned by the city of Boulder, a natural reservoir for its water supply.

Fire as well as ice formed the Rockies' scenery, including the volcanic Never Summer Range, just west of the Front Range in Rocky Mountain National Park, and the mighty San Juan Mountains of southern Colorado. About 40 million years ago, during a particularly active buckling of the earth, volcanoes broke to the surface over much of the state. From deep within the earth, gold, silver, and other valuable minerals were carried to the surface, eventually to spawn innumerable mines and legacies of ghost towns. This fiery altering of the Colorado landscape went on for nearly 30 million years.

Easily visible from a Salt Lake City–bound airplane are large reservoirs just west of the Front Range. These lakes are in Middle Park, one of four large intermountain valleys in Colorado. (The others are the San Luis Valley, South Park, and North Park. In Colorado, the word *park* is used to describe a valley containing few trees and surrounded by forested mountains.) Not every piece of land went up during the buckling of North America. Some blocks slipped down, including not only the four big valleys but many smaller ones as well.

And some blocks were forced up but did not tilt; sed-

floors at the headwalls, it froze. As the ice moved, the rock frozen to it was plucked from the walls.

Thus, glaciers formed semicircular cliffs and basins—cirques—at the heads of valleys. Lakes often are contained in cirques where glaciers dug holes on the basin floors. Or lakes may lie behind the natural dams of glacial moraines, the ridges of rock and earth dumped by glaciers where they melted. Glacier-formed lakes usually are found also in the valleys below the cirques.

The rock in moraines is rubble from glacial plucking

imentary rock that covers western Colorado remains essentially horizontal. Various parts of this plateau country were lifted higher than others and all were lifted at least a mile. The rise in elevation did not give much slant to the landscape, but the extra altitude did increase the erosive power of the Colorado River and its tributaries. This, plus a very dry climate that prevented growth of many erosion-retarding plants, resulted in a landscape dominated by deep, steep canyons.

Nearly all of Colorado is very dry compared with the Mississippi River states and those farther east. Colorado residents have to adjust to a climate that never seems to provide enough water. Sensitivity to aridity can create unique attitudes toward the weather. Nice days are gray and rainy; grumbling is heard about yet another disappointing day of blue skies and sunshine.

The flatlands that encompass the eastern third of Colorado are too dry to support natural tree growth except along frequently dusty streambeds. Over this expansive grass-covered habitat once roamed herds of bison and the colorful Indian tribes who hunted them. The serpentine South Platte and its tributaries etch the plains of northern Colorado while flowing to the Missouri. One hundred miles to the south, the Arkansas River and its feeder streams wind toward the Mississippi. Many reservoirs spangle the plains to retard the exit of water from Colorado.

The plains are dry because they lie in the rain shadow of the Rockies, a 140-mile-wide barrier to the moisture carried by prevailing Pacific winds. Even on clear days, wisps of clouds usually hang about the peaks where air masses must rise to clear the mountains. Moisture-laden air moves into cooler temperatures as it rises and no longer can hold as much water. Water vapor condenses to form clouds, then rain or snow.

Because cooling and cloud formation occur as the air rises, most of the rain and snow are dumped on the western side of the mountains. The unmarked line of the continental divide snakes along glacier-sculptured ridges and peaks, arbitrarily decreeing that most of the water from mountains' western slopes will end up in the

The volcanic Sneffels Range rises above irrigated hayfields. More than $125 million in precious metals has been mined from this part of the San Juan Mountains.

Amid glaciated valleys and cirques in Indian Peaks Wilderness, the continental divide wanders to its easternmost point on Sawtooth Mountain. To the right are Winter Park and Middle Park.

Colorado River instead of the Platte or Arkansas.

Along some stretches of the mountains, the continental divide is relatively easy to see. Clearly visible are drainage patterns indicating that water which falls on one side of the divide flows west, while water which falls on the other side flows east. In other places, the tortuous meanderings of the continental divide are well camouflaged among the peaks and passes.

The great bulk of Colorado's population lives east of the continental divide. The great bulk of Colorado's water is on the western side of the divide. Large reservoirs on the western slope capture precious water until it can be diverted to the east. Other reservoirs are intended to hold water within the state so that it can be used to irrigate western-slope hayfields and orchards.

Recreation is governed by the distribution of water. Since most of the snow falls west of the divide, most of the big ski resorts are there. It is necessary to transport most skiers from east to west, just as it is necessary to transport melted snow in the opposite direction. Like some of the water, some of the skiers go through the mountains in tunnels. Ski trains chug through the Moffat Railroad Tunnel to deposit skiers conveniently at Winter Park's slopes. Many more skiers are funneled through Eisenhower Tunnel on Interstate Highway 70, portal to many ski resorts—Copper Mountain, Breckenridge, Keystone, Vail, Aspen, to name only a few.

Summer recreation in the mountains is less dependent on water distribution, in part because that distribution has been rearranged by diversion projects. Most mountain enthusiasts play on the sunnier eastern slope. Obviously, however, the bulk of white-water rafting takes place in the Colorado River drainage. Most of the exciting stretches of river always have been on the west of the divide, but dams have eliminated much of this popular recreation resource.

Convenience dictates that most hiking and backpacking are done on the handy eastern slope of Front Range

Above: *In the San Luis Valley desert, wind piles sand 700 feet high within Great Sand Dunes National Monument.*

Below: *Stone stumps at Florissant Fossil Beds are sequoias buried by volcanic ash 35 million years ago.*

national forests and Rocky Mountain National Park. However, more rain means lusher vegetation on the western slope. Walkers west of the divide enjoy more profuse explosions of wildflower color. And they are privileged to encounter more deer, elk, bighorn sheep, and other wildlife species that feed on the plants. More cameras than packs are carried along Colorado trails, and the west-slope peaks have more snow with which to accent scenic vistas in summer. Similarly, the clear, rushing mountain streams so popular with hikers are kept rushing longer where there are more melting snow-banks to feed the streams.

The abundant recreational resources of Rocky Mountain country lure Colorado residents and visitors to both sides of the mountains throughout the year. Nearly everyone wants to experience the state. But most are surprised when they discover the great range of stimulating and interesting experiences available because of Colorado's great diversity.

Two Thousand Years to Statehood

Harassment by hostile Indians, voting practices of dubious legality, mysterious lost communities built on cliffs above the desert—the summer of 1874 turned out to be rather interesting for William H. Jackson.

Chief photographer for the federal scientific survey of the West led by Ferdinand V. Hayden between 1869 and 1878, Jackson had disturbed originally cooperative Utes. Rumor spread among them that his bulky camera would cause sickness. A less-than-subtle marksmanship demonstration prevented an Indian attack, but a cold-war standoff could produce few good photos of the Utes. Jackson took his camera crew and hustled away from Ute wrath.

Retreating to the southwest corner of Colorado, Jackson's crew encountered a miner named John Moss who said he could help the photographer salvage a generally disappointing summer. Nearby, on Mesa Verde—Spanish for "green table"—Moss had seen a large number of cliff dwellings. Abandoned long before the Spanish had arrived in the 1500s, these cliff dwellings were little known and never had been photographed.

Moss volunteered to guide Jackson's crew to the ruins, but the practical miner needed their help in return. As Jackson later wrote in his autobiography, *Time Exposure,* "Our host and guide was a candidate for some political office in the new and sparsely settled County of Rio Grande, and since the residence requirements were on the sketchy side for this first election, it was an easy matter for my photographic party, including the boys, to help vote him into office. After our ballots had been cast Moss closed the polls, and we were off."

Deep shadows filled Mancos Canyon, cut in the flank of Mesa Verde, when the photographic explorers rode in at dusk on September 9. Moss gestured toward the top of a cliff to indicate a ruin. In the gloom, it was difficult to see a two-story wall the same color as the sandstone niche into which it was tucked. Dark windows helped to distinguish the cliff dwelling from the cliff.

Unwilling to put off investigation until morning, the group scrambled up the 600-foot canyon wall only to be stymied by a seemingly smooth cliff 50 feet short of the ruin. Most quit until morning, but Jackson and an accompanying journalist named Ernest Ingersoll refused to give up. Wrestling a dead pine up to the wall, they propped it in place as a ladder. This raised them to ancient footholds and handholds cut in the rock, the cliff dwellers' route that had been invisible in the twilight.

"It was worth everything I possessed," Jackson wrote in *Time Exposure,* "to stand there and know that, with Ernest Ingersoll, I was surely the first white man who had ever looked down into the canyon from this dwelling in the cliff." Taking many photos and notes, Jackson discovered dozens of ruins that peppered the Mesa Verde area. Many were nearly intact, well preserved by the dry climate. Soon most of the world knew of one of America's greatest historic treasures.

In 1906, Mesa Verde's fame caused it to become the first historic site to be preserved in a national park. More recent history can be enjoyed in Colorado at National Park Service living-history programs at Bent's Old Fort National Historic Site and Never Summer Ranch in Rocky Mountain National Park. Many mining-boom mansions are preserved in Colorado, while more modest buildings slowly decay in innumerable ghost towns. Narrow-gauge railroads built to serve the mines now haul tourists into the nineteenth century amid spectacular vistas. But Mesa Verde remains the most fascinating of the state's historic attractions.

The lure of Mesa Verde's mysterious mood, plus valuable relics to be found, inspired exploration by local ranchers. In 1888, Richard Wetherill and Charlie Mason located a huge ruin sheltered in a deep enclave four miles up a side canyon from where Jackson had found his "Two-Story Cliff House." The cowboys called their

Square Tower House has the tallest structure in Mesa Verde National Park. Found by Wetherill and Mason the day after they discovered Cliff Palace, it contains about 70 rooms.

discovery, the largest of Mesa Verde's cliff communities, Cliff Palace.

In the following years Wetherill explored a great many Indian ruins in the San Juan River Basin, where Arizona, New Mexico, Utah, and Colorado meet—the Four Corners. Trying to part the curtain of mystery that hung over all the ruins, Wetherill asked Navajos and Utes, "Who lived in these houses? Why did they leave?" But the nomadic Utes and Navajos could not answer. "They were the Anasazi," the Navajos said, "the Ancient Ones."

Archaeologists following Wetherill, however, have been able to piece together a rather complete story of the Anasazi. About 2,000 years ago, nomadic Indians in the San Juan basin picked up farming practices spreading north from Mexico. They learned to grow corn and squash, and settled down to live in one place. Given a reliable food source and relieved of the necessity of foraging for their next meal, the Anasazi quickly developed a much richer culture.

Over the next thousand years, they developed fine basketry followed by even better pottery. Beans, cotton, and melons were added to their crops. They domesticated turkeys. The bow and arrow were invented. Architecture expanded, specialized, and finally culminated in the great Cliff Palace, built around A.D. 1175.

Hauling cumbersome cameras on a mule, William H. Jackson (left) photographed the Utes, who adapted their Plains culture to mountain parks. Chief Peah posed in front of his tipi but turned hostile and futilely demanded the negatives the next day. Colorado Historical Society.

Pressure from hungry nomads wandering in from the north, probably Navajo and Apache peoples, caused the Anasazi to construct cliff communities. These defensive precautions kept the invaders at bay. Ill-fed nomads could not drive hundreds of healthy and organized farmers from their fortified homes.

A drought from 1276 to 1299, together with nomad raids, has been blamed for the Anasazis' abandoning their homes and fields. But it is doubtful that the drought could have been so catastrophic as to drive out all the farmers. Some ruins were deserted before the drought.

Through the centuries, the Anasazi population probably expanded to exceed the number of people who live in the Four Corners today. Overpopulation put so much pressure on their environment that it no longer could support Indian farmers.

They had to cut down many trees (the growth rings of which give us very exact dates for Four Corners events) to build houses and cook food for so many people. When forests were destroyed, their roots no longer held the scant precipitation on the land to be released slowly in springs. Instead water ran off quickly, carrying with it fertile soil, much of which had been formed in a wet glacial climate 10,000 years before. Erosion lowered the level of natural streams and irrigation ditches so that it was more difficult to irrigate fields. Repeated irrigation reduced soil fertility by concentrating salts and leaching out nutrients.

The sophisticated people who built Cliff Palace, who crafted extremely artistic ceramics, may have guessed what was happening to them. But their society could not prevent the sacrifice of long-term needs in the pursuit of short-term needs. As a result, the whole Anasazi livelihood deteriorated.

Farmers with the least productive fields or less advantageous homes felt the pressure first. They moved away to seek a better place. Bit by bit desertion continued. Then came the 24-year drought, destroying already depleted crop yields. When it ended in 1300, only the wind and wildlife lived at Mesa Verde.

Ute, Navajo, and Apache nomads drifted into the land the Anasazi vacated. Using dogs to haul their few possessions, these wanderers followed the seasonal migrations of bison and other game animals, as well as the seasonal fruiting of wild edible plants. The nomads lived in uneasy equilibrium with Anasazi descendants in New Mexico and Arizona, sometimes raiding the farmers, sometimes trading hides for agricultural products.

In a futile search for gold, the Spanish explorer Francisco Vásquez de Coronado marched north from Mexico in 1541 and met Indian farmers and nomads. Other Spaniards followed, and they reintroduced horses to North America. During the Ice Ages, modern horses had wandered between North America and Asia over a land bridge in the area of the Bering Sea. Melting of continental glaciers raised the sea level and drowned the bridge. Prehistoric North Americans then killed off two-thirds of the large mammal species, including horses. During the intervening 7,000 years horses had dropped from the Indians' cultural memory.

Spanish conquistadors reintroduced horses as domestic animals and taught the Pueblo Indians of New Mexico that horses were good for something besides food. But, as sedentary farmers, the Pueblos had little use for equestrian skills. They had even less use for their Spanish conquerors and drove them out for 13 years, between 1680 and 1693. During the Pueblo revolt, the Spanish lost many horses.

Pueblos traded these steeds north and east. When nomads obtained horses by trade or theft, there occurred as dramatic a cultural revolution as the world ever has known. Indian mobility was greatly increased and hunting bison became easy. Freed from spending most of their time looking for food, the newly mounted nomads spent their leisure making war on Indian farmers, whites, and other nomads.

From the early 1700s to mid-1800s, the plains of Colorado were a battleground of constantly warring tribes trying to expand their range into the sunbelt plains, original source of horses and home to millions of bison. Playing power politics in an arena where they had little military power to match that of the Indians, the Spanish sometimes interfered in these Indian wars. But, aside from Spanish names scattered across southern Colorado, they had little influence. More influential were the French, who provided guns to the hunting, warring Plains Indians.

First the Apaches battled with the Utes; then both were overwhelmed by the Comanches, who finally were driven south of the Arkansas River by Cheyennes and Arapahos in 1838. The whites who inadvertently began this process by supplying horses and guns ultimately seized control in the 1860s.

In 1806, Lt. Zebulon Pike entered Colorado to explore the southern limits of the United States' 1803 Louisiana Purchase. He tried to climb the 14,110-foot mountain that later was named Pikes Peak, but his experience in the East had ill-prepared him for the scale of the West. The "Great Mountain" was too high to ascend in November snows. Most of the rest of Pike's time in Colorado was spent exploring the southern part of the state. Actually, his travels are most accurately described as getting more and more lost.

Finally, Pike's party of explorers was picked up by the Spanish and shipped home by a roundabout route. In 1810, Pike published an account of his exploration, which stimulated American interest in Colorado mountains as a source of beaver furs for making hats and in the Colorado plains as a highway to rich trading with Santa Fe. The War of 1812 occupied the nation's attention until 1815. But renewed interest in potential wealth to be trapped in Colorado beaver ponds caused the federal government in 1820 to send Maj. Stephen Long to get more facts.

Long's expedition accomplished a number of firsts. His artist, Samuel Seymour, produced the first view of the Rockies, a painting from near Fort Morgan of the preeminent peak of the Front Range, which eventually would be named Longs Peak. The group's naturalist, Titian Peale, executed the first drawings of Indian tipis and many types of wildlife. Long's botanist, Edwin James, discovered (among various other plants) the blue columbine, eventually to be designated Colorado's state flower. James also achieved the first ascent of a 14,000-foot peak in North America by a white man. He made it up Pikes Peak, only to discover on his descent that his untended campfire had started the first forest fire ignited by a white man in the Rockies.

For several years before Long set out, American merchants had been trying to trade cheap U.S.-manufactured goods for silver and furs in Santa Fe. But Spanish colonial policy decreed that all goods for Santa Fe had to pass through the Mexican port of Vera Cruz and then over a long mule-train route fraught with hardship and great danger. After the Mexican Revolution removed Spanish control, beleaguered Santa Fe consumers in 1821 joyously opened New Mexico to traders from St. Louis. St. Louis was only 780 miles away, most of it comparatively easy terrain. The savings in transport made American goods much cheaper, and they soon dominated the Santa Fe market.

By 1828, hundreds of wagons rolled along the Santa Fe Trail, which followed the Arkansas River, and then over Raton Pass along the route of Interstate Highway 25. The trail's Cimarron Cutoff across the southeast corner of Colorado avoided the mountains around Raton by facing grim deserts and grimmer Comanches. But the rewards of the Santa Fe trade were worth the dangers and trials of the trail: Americans returned to Missouri with hundreds of thousands of dollars' worth of silver and beaver pelts.

In 1833, Bent, St. Vrain & Company, a partnership of very experienced fur traders, built Bent's Fort on the Raton Pass branch of the Santa Fe Trail, near modern La Junta. Well located to exploit both the Santa Fe trade and Indian trade, this adobe castle allowed Charles and William Bent and Ceran St. Vrain to dominate Colorado in the 1830s and 1840s. Through Bent's Fort passed the bulk of the wealth in beaver fur produced in Colorado.

Beaver lost its importance in the late 1830s because of overtrapping and competition from larger nutria pelts from the Amazon basin. The final blow was development of silk hats. Bent, St. Vrain & Company simply switched their trade to buffalo hides. Bison were not commercially wiped out in Colorado until 30 years after declining trade and cholera forced William Bent to abandon his fort in 1849.

Bent's Fort was filled with manufactured goods needed by Plains Indians. Through honest dealings, shrewd economic diplomacy, relation by marriage of the Bents to the Cheyennes, and an impregnable military position, the company enforced an unsteady truce among warring tribes who came to trade hides. Indians did their trading through a secure double gate in the fort's walls. That such security was necessary was indicated by an 1839 raid in which 20 Comanches ran off horses that had been grazing outside the walls, leaving in exchange three arrows in a dead herdsman.

Inside the fort, where the Bents ruled like kings, numerous company employees, men such as Kit Carson, guaranteed the trading post's safety. Also present was a constantly shifting population of unaffiliated mountain men as experienced as Carson but who chose to remain free of any man's employ. Some had endured two decades of seeking beaver in the Rockies, as totally free and colorful as any individuals in American history. Always in danger of death from accident, natural hazards, and Indians, many eventually succumbed to these perils.

But some survived to lead such army explorers as John Fremont and John Gunnison through the moun-tains. Others would help secure the Rockies by force of arms. Bent's Fort was a staging ground in 1846 for the taking of New Mexico by an American army under Stephen Watts Kearny. William Bent led.Kearny's scouts. Kearny named Charles Bent the American governor of New Mexico, an appointment that ended in Bent's murder in Taos in an 1847 revolt. Ceran St. Vrain led a company of volunteers that helped reestablish American control after bloody fighting.

After Utes wiped out traders at Fort Pueblo, Colorado, in 1854, Kit Carson led federal troops in a punitive expedition that eliminated danger from Indians in the southern part of the state. Fort Garland was established

Bent's Old Fort National Historic Site owes its strategic location on the Arkansas River to trade moving along the Santa Fe Trail. Cannon atop corner bastions made the adobe castle impregnable.

Central City blanketed Gregory Gulch soon after gold was discovered in 1859, eclipsing Denver as the area's most important community. Central City's $67 million in gold funded a substantial number of buildings, such as the Teller House hotel, built in 1872 for $107,000.

in 1858 to prevent Ute raids; Carson commanded there in 1866–67. Tom "Broken Hand" Fitzpatrick's reputation as a mountain man gained him an Indian agent job, and he managed to delay war with the Cheyennes and Arapahos by negotiating a treaty in 1851.

The era of mountain men and Indians ended in 1858. In that year, gold-seeking Cherokees from Indian Territory and white prospectors from Georgia hit pay dirt at the junction of Cherry Creek and the South Platte River, now downtown Denver. News of this discovery exploded in an America suffering from the financial panic of 1857. Hordes of men with nothing to lose headed west in a boom similar to the 1849 California gold rush. Between 1858 and 1860, Colorado's non-Indian population jumped from about 200 to almost 35,000.

Initial Colorado strikes proved to be unimpressive, and many argonauts returned to the East bitterly disappointed. Just as they left, really big strikes were made near Central City and Idahoe Bar (later called Idaho Springs). The boom began again.

For the rest of the century, boom followed bust as one precious mineral strike after another gave Colorado's economy a roller-coaster ride. Played-out mines, ore refining problems, oversupplied markets, labor violence, and transportation difficulties made mineral extraction an unstable base on which to build a society.

But the glitter of gold and silver did not blind everyone to less tangible values. Among the first gold seekers to arrive in 1858 was 20-year-old Julia Holmes, a pioneer woman with independent ideas. Refusing to wear long dresses, Julia wore a knee-length skirt with bloomers underneath. Told that she looked odd in this costume, she maintained that freedom to move about was more important than fashion. The indomitable Mrs. Holmes emphasized her point by accompanying her husband to the top of Pikes Peak on August 5, 1858, the first woman to climb to over 14,000 feet in North America.

Upright miners were determined that not all mining camps would be hell-raisin' dens of iniquity. Before formal government caught up with the gold rush, miners set up mining districts to perform the functions of counties. Many districts prohibited such things as "bawdy houses, grog shops, gamboling saloons," and professional lawyers.

In 1859, more official law and order was deemed desirable. Some of the mining districts were in Kansas Territory, some in Nebraska Territory. All were too far west to interest territorial governors concerned with pre–Civil War politics. So miners formed their own Territory of Jefferson and elected Beverly D. Williams to convince Congress to confirm and fund the new territorial government.

President Jefferson had secured the Rockies for the United States through the Louisiana Purchase. But antislavery forces dominating the House of Representatives were not enthusiastic about a new territory named after a slaveholding Virginian. Others pointed out that there already was a Washington Territory, and the first president "stood alone in his glory."

Tired of hearing nothing from the nation's capital about the Territory of Jefferson, self-proclaimed government-makers met again and created Idaho Territory, named for the site of the first big gold strike. They elected a new delegate to Congress, and also sent representatives to Omaha, Nebraska, and Lawrence, Kansas (it was a confusing time). Soon other miners got together to exercise the American talent for self-government and sent their own delegates to Congress.

In February, 1861, Texas seceded from the Union, joining the rest of the Deep South. This brought rebellion too close to Rocky Mountain treasure houses. Also, the swelling army of delegates to Congress from the gold fields intensified their assault on the capitol building. Congress had to pay attention to setting up government for . . . whatever that territory out West was.

One of the territorial lobbyists, George M. Willing, told his fellow lobbyists that Idaho was an Indian word for "gem of the mountains." The truth was that Idaho was not an Indian name but was being put forward as a choice that would not offend anyone. Idaho had strong backing in the House of Representatives.

B. D. Williams, lobbying on the Senate side of Congress, switched his support from Jefferson to Idaho until he found out that Idaho really had no meaning. He then demanded a switch to Colorado, Spanish for "colored red." Colorado describes the volcanic San Juan Mountains that the Spanish had known and also the sedimentary rock slabs leaning against the Front Range.

Meanwhile, other names came up in the House, including Tampa, Colona, Osage, San Juan, Nemara,

Weapollea, and Lulu. These all were rejected. It was, after all, an obvious step down from Jefferson to Lulu. The House committee considering this vital question while the nation literally was falling apart finally settled on the name Tahosa, which really was an Indian word—Kiowa for "Dwellers of the Mountain Tops." The Senate version, however, won out. Colorado Territory was created February 28, 1861.

The regional self-esteem adopted by new Colorado residents today was evident also in the 1860s. Motivated partly by a desire to make money from a growing population and partly by sincere pride, vociferous, ever-optimistic, and occasionally daffy boosters heralded Colorado's climate, beauty, and agricultural potential, as well as its remarkably progressive and noble citizens.

Leader among the boosters was William N. Byers, pioneer editor of Denver's *Rocky Mountain News*, who founded the newspaper in 1859. His editorial stands were neither timid nor moderate, and guns were kept handy to the printing press. A real-estate developer as well as an editor, Byers promoted a health spa at Hot Sulphur Springs and agricultural colonies based on irrigation.

Byers, an excellent fisherman, extolled the outdoor life for which Colorado is still famous. In 1864, he failed at his first attempt to ascend Longs Peak, speculating that wings might be necessary to reach the top of this prominent landmark. But in 1868, the editor was in the first party on top, led by one-armed John Wesley Powell, who later led the first Colorado River exploration through the Grand Canyon.

If Byers's ambitions for Colorado were lofty, those of William Gilpin were stellar. Appointed first territorial governor in 1861 by President Abraham Lincoln, Gilpin was qualified by virtue of 18 years' exciting experience in the West. However, Gilpin had a remarkable capacity to ignore the facts of his experiences if they did not happen to support his mystical vision of Colorado as the hub of a new and glorious world civilization. Given to extravagant exaggeration and endless oration, his descriptions of Colorado made heaven seem a rather poor place by comparison.

Governor Gilpin's unrestrained enthusiasm led him into unauthorized spending for territorial organization and defense. Lincoln removed him after less than a year

in office. Even Byers, who was at least sympathetic, regarded Gilpin as "a very peculiar man."

Gilpin's main theme, however, was totally accurate—the need for railroads to develop Colorado's potential. Many Colorado citizens realized this truth, but the man who did the most about it was William Jackson Palmer. Founder of the Denver & Rio Grande Railroad, Palmer drove his narrow-gauge line (the tracks were only three feet apart) into awesome mountain terrain to bring out precious metals. It was said that if a farmer had a wagonload of pumpkins, Palmer would build a railroad across the mountains to carry them to market.

A social visionary as well as a railroad tycoon, Palmer founded Colorado Springs in 1871 as a carefully designed resort, proving that good taste and appreciation of beauty could be profitable. In Pueblo, Palmer organized in 1880 the Colorado Coal and Iron Company (later Colorado Fuel and Iron Company) to supply coal and rails for western railroads.

Although Colorado boosters did a good job of providing the trappings of civilization in relatively short order, statehood remained an elusive goal for political reasons. Finally, Colorado was admitted to the Union because Republicans in Congress could be sure that the new state's three electoral votes would be cast for presidential candidate Rutherford B. Hayes. Colorado became the thirty-eighth state on August 1, 1876, as the nation celebrated its hundredth birthday. The "Centennial State" cast its electoral votes as promised. Hayes gained the presidency by one electoral vote.

Colorado was vital to another 1876 political goal when the federal survey run by Ferdinand V. Hayden set out to impress visitors to the Philadelphia Centennial Exposition with the wonders of the West. Hayden reasoned that centennial-celebrating citizens would then pressure Congress to fund continued work by Hayden's explorers who discovered the wonders.

Hayden put William Henry Jackson in charge of this lobbying effort. Jackson's photos of Mount of the Holy Cross, one of Colorado's most awesome 14,000-foot peaks, already had uplifted American spiritual feelings after he revealed its cross-etched face in 1873. At the Centennial Exposition, Jackson's photos won seven medals and much esteem for the Hayden Survey.

But even more alluring were scale models Jackson

Mount of the Holy Cross is hidden by surrounding peaks, which adds to its spiritual impact. Thousands of pilgrims have climbed Notch Mountain for this view.

made of Anasazi cliff dwellings he had discovered in 1874. These, plus geological samples and Indian artifacts collected by the survey, achieved their purpose. Hayden managed to extract enough money from Congress to keep his efforts going for two more years.

Centennial Exposition visitors extracted from Jackson tales about Indians, cliff dwellings, mountain men, the taste of buffalo hump, the geology of Colorado mining, and glorious adventure amid Colorado scenery. The Hayden Survey exhibit focused national attention on the whole span of history that had brought the Centennial State into being. National interest in Colorado has not slackened since.

Treasure Trove of the Rockies

"There was no smoke rising from the chimneys. It was a true deserted village, another ghost town. Prospect holes, ore dumps, and the rúins of three stamp mills bespoke its origin—and its end. But though we searched for an hour we found no trace of evidence to tell us the dead town's name, or who had lived there, or when."

William Henry Jackson's description in *Time Exposure* of his 1873 encounter with a Colorado ghost town betrays a fascination with towns that sprang up and died like grotesque fungi, fostered by lust for quick and easy riches. Old mining towns continue to be one of the state's main attractions more than a century later.

When Jackson stumbled onto his deserted village, Colorado Territory already had experienced two booms and busts since gold first was discovered in 1858. Jackson arrived in the midst of yet another boom to take pictures for the U.S. Department of the Interior. He was part of the Hayden Survey, which was scientifically mapping the natural resources of the Colorado Rockies. By the time a summary of the survey was published in 1877, the new state's mining economy had had another decline. But mining was about to boom again.

Ferdinand Hayden's summary, *Atlas of Colorado*, which clearly indicated all the geologically promising places to look for more mineral wealth, did much to help that boom along. The mining belt the Hayden Survey outlined is a 50-mile wide band through the mountains from Ward, northwest of Boulder, almost to the southwest corner of the state. Today most of the recoverable precious minerals have been extracted. What remains is the mother lode of Colorado's visitor attractions.

Central City is Colorado's most famous mining town. Established in 1859 as part of Colorado's first major gold discovery, it contains the finest collection of nineteenth-century commercial buildings in the state. These rise above winding streets jammed into Gregory Gulch, touted as the richest square mile on earth.

In summer, Central City swarms with visitors patronizing shops, historic restorations, and the outstanding Central City Opera House, built in 1878 and still featuring very fine performances. Some folks complain that an inexplicit "they" have ruined Central City by exploiting its past to mine the billfolds of visiting tourists. Certainly, Central City summer can be tawdry and crowded beyond the point of pleasantness. It thus recreates with near perfection its original boomtown mood. Many old mining towns in Colorado are quaint, charming, and thoroughly pleasant. Central City, on the other hand, is authentic; everyone should experience it sometime.

Most Central City gold was locked in quartz ore that had to be crushed and processed for the gold to be removed. Mills to do this were very expensive, and gold mining required much more start-up capital than the cost of a pick and pan. Moreover, before 1869 in Colorado, it was not understood how to do this efficiently. Only ores containing an exceptionally high percentage of gold could be milled profitably.

Therefore, Colorado mining was in a bust cycle in 1869, when the Boston and Colorado smelter opened in Black Hawk, adjacent to Central City. Based on a combination of New England investment and technical expertise imported from Europe, the Black Hawk smelter demonstrated how to make mining profitable; the boom was on again. The mill was kept busy night and day, filling the narrow valley of Clear Creek with clouds of noxious sulfur dioxide. Arrival of Colorado's first narrow-gauge railroad in 1872 made the Central City–Blackhawk Mining District even more profitable.

On summer weekends, recreational gold panners line the banks of Clear Creek below Black Hawk. More serious though still small-scale attempts are made with today's technology to recover even more gold from low-grade ores that the previous milling missed.

At Idaho Springs, placer gold (particles released from the main ore body by centuries of natural erosion and

Fireweed blooms where buildings once burned in Cripple Creek. Trains brought coal to the bins above, near a brick station now converted to a mining-district museum.

In 1859, George Griffith founded Georgetown after reaching Central City too late to stake a rich gold claim.

Opposite page: *Although gold seekers still pan Clear Creek 124 years later (top), silver was the metal that fueled the Georgetown boom and such architectural potpourri as private home Maxwell House (bottom).*

mixed by water in deposits of sand and gravel) was found by George Jackson in 1859. Always alert for flecks of "color," Jackson discovered the gold when he was watching a herd of mountain sheep attracted to hot springs. This discovery eventually yielded millions of dollars in placer gold and began Colorado's mining heritage. As in Central City, however, the easy pickings of placer gold soon gave out. Large capital investment in gold mills was necessary. The huge Argo Mill closed in 1943 but today offers tours to explain the process of crushing gold-bearing ore and extracting the valuable metal. Hot springs that soothed tired miners in 1859 still bubble up today, providing the same relief to road-weary tourists or battered skiers.

Georgetown was the "Silver Queen" after 1864,

when Colorado's first large silver discovery was made about five miles away. An efficient volunteer fire department and some good luck kept Georgetown from burning to the ground like most other Colorado mining camps. More than 200 original buildings are still clustered in Georgetown, the state's premier collection of mining-town residences.

The Georgetown Society conducts tours through its Hamill House, the mansion of silver baron William Hamill, restored to its original opulence. Hamill House typifies the residence of a truly successful man, complete with a six-hole gingerbread outhouse—three walnut holes on one side of a partition for the family, three pine seats on the opposite side for servants.

You also can visit restored Hotel De Paris, built in 1875 by Frenchman Louis Depuy to serve the business generated by $200 million worth of silver extracted from nearby mines. A narrow-gauge railroad over the serpentine route of the Georgetown Loop takes visitors to a tour of the Lebanon Mine and Mill and on up to another old mining town, Silver Plume. But the main fascination of Georgetown is less in specific historic sites and tours than in one street after another of private homes restored to period elegance. Nowhere is the Western adaptation of various "revival" styles of Victorian architecture better displayed.

The rush to the Rockies begun in 1859 created additional mining camps along the Blue River, places such as Dillon (the original site now drowned under Dillon Reservoir), Silverthorne, and Frisco. Breckenridge was named after Vice-President John C. Breckinridge. In 1861, to demonstrate their sympathy for the Union cause, the town's residents repudiated the former vice-president, who had cast his lot with the Confederacy, and changed the spelling of their town's name by substituting an "e" for an "i." Breckenridge has preserved much of its mining-town heritage in restored buildings. It cannot get rid of another aspect of that heritage— waterways permanently scarred by dredges scouring out gold in the first part of the twentieth century. All of these towns also display much modern ski-resort architecture built to serve superb nearby slopes.

The 1859 mining boom sprouted many mining towns in South Park. Most are only memories. But Fairplay contains the South Park City Museum, a reconstruction of a nineteenth-century Colorado town made up of buildings salvaged from nearby decaying mining camps. Furnished with early Colorado artifacts, the town contains a railroad depot with narrow-gauge train, newspaper office, drugstore, saloon, assay office, and general store.

Across the Mosquito Range from Fairplay, near the headwaters of the Arkansas River, still another fabulously rich gold strike was made in 1860 in California Gulch. But these placer mines were barely producing anything by 1873 when "Uncle Billy" Stevens figured out that there was silver in the lead carbonate in California Gulch. The information was kept secret for a remarkably long time while Uncle Billy hired miners to dig what he described as lead ore. But by 1877 an international rush was on to Leadville that made the 1859 boom seem tame indeed.

Today Leadville is the nation's highest incorporated city, approximately 10,200 feet above sea level. Just south of town, easily visible above the Victorian rooftops, are Mount Elbert (14,433 feet) and Mount Massive (14,421 feet), first and second in altitude in Colorado. Since 1860, the area has produced $700 million in a variety of valuable minerals. The bulk of this wealth was the silver that made Leadville a roaring boomtown in the 1880s. More recently lead, zinc, and molybdenum have bolstered the area's mining tradition.

The downtown area has been redeveloped to resemble the flush, high-spending days of the 1880s. Then tourists visited Leadville to catch a glimpse of such fascinating silver barons as Horace Tabor, a diamond stickpin on his chest and beautiful Baby Doe on his arm. Tabor scandalized Colorado when he divorced his loyal but plain wife, Augusta, and married Baby Doe in Washington, D.C., in a wedding bash that was remarkable for its ostentatious display of Horace's great wealth. Such prodigious spending funded the Tabor Opera House in Leadville and an even grander theater in Denver. Tabor had a great talent for investing in silver mines, which eventually yielded him $26 million. He spent it all and was wiped out when the United States converted from bimetal support for its currency to the gold standard in 1893.

Horace Tabor died in 1899. On his deathbed, he told Baby Doe, "Hang onto the Matchless," his best Leadville mine, which had yielded at times $100,000 per month. "It will make millions again," he predicted.

It did not. But Baby Doe lived in a mine shack at the Matchless in rags and sacks until 1935. She froze to death there one winter night, repenting the ways of her youth. Thousands of Leadville tourists have trooped through the shack, gazed down into the shaft of the Matchless, and contemplated this tragedy of Shakespearean proportions.

Leadville has many other restored historic sites and museums. Probably the one to visit first for background is the Heritage Museum. Next door is Healy House, maintained by the Historical Society of Colorado. This first substantial Victorian home in Leadville was built in 1878 and is restored to duplicate 1899. The guides for this home and the adjacent Dexter Cabin are costumed and take the roles of schoolteachers who boarded in the house in 1899. They are firm in their determination not to break character, and they speak in the present tense whenever answering questions about Leadville's history. This stepping back into 1899 is disconcerting to many visitors, who feel uncomfortable with let's-pretend no matter how informative the game may be.

The guides tell a story (on their lunch hour, when characters can be dropped) of a visitor who got grumpy over the whole thing. Finally, at the end of the 45-minute tour, he stomped out of the house and encountered the woman whose gardening wizardry at over 10,000 feet makes the grounds of Healy House a horticultural showplace. At the time, she was cutting the lawn with an electric mower.

Glaring at the mower, the visitor blared out, "And I suppose that's eighteen ninety-nine, too."

"Yes," the gardener answered, never breaking stride, "and worth every penny of it!"

Some of the incredible wealth generated by Leadville mines funneled into Twin Lakes, the resort community where Leadville millionaires retreated from the cares of getting rich. Lodges, hotels, and cabins dotted the lakes' shores, and there was talk of importing Venetian-style gondolas. The promoters of this idea were unsure of how many boats to purchase, and asked millionaire miner John Morrissey how many gondolas he thought were needed. Morrissey suggested that they "just get a couple and let 'em breed."

Costumed as 1899 schoolteachers, Healy House guides play croquet on the lawn of the restored Leadville home.

Not all Leadville millionaires were as ignorant and unrefined as Morrissey. When the Twin Lakes were dammed, trees and shrubs along the lakes were destroyed, and water level fluctuated at the will of the dam owners. Disgusted with this "uglification," many wealthy folks moved away.

Successful miners could soak away their cares at Mount Princeton Hot Springs, near Buena Vista, still popular with hot-water enthusiasts today. Farther up the road is the near ghost town of St. Elmo, one of the most photogenic of the old mining camps. Gold and silver miners picked up supplies here from 1880 until 1926, when the narrow-gauge railroad tracks were taken up for lack of business. There still is abundant gold, for the road to St. Elmo is one of the best places in Colorado to witness aspen gold in autumn.

Aspen obviously are abundant around the town named for them. But it was the rock formations revealed by Hayden's atlas, similar to those around Leadville, that drew miners over Independence Pass in 1879. On the upper reaches of the stream that Hayden had labelled Roaring Fork, Aspen eventually was second only to Leadville in the production of silver. Refugees from the perpetual sinning at Leadville were determined that Aspen would be different. To a large degree they were successful in keeping the town tame.

Modern Aspen is one of America's most famous and glamorous ski towns. In summer, when masses of wildflowers spring up in response to melting snow, Aspen remains lively as a cultural center. The quality of its artists is unexcelled, as is the beauty of setting in which they perform. Aspen contains many fine restored Victorian buildings that form an interesting counterpoint to the nearby ghost town of Ashcroft, a silver-mining community that died from lack of rail service, which reached Aspen in 1887. The ruins of Ashcroft are not restored, but they have been more or less stabilized, suspending the town's sentence of death carried out by wind, snow, decay, and vandals.

Also convenient to Aspen are some of Colorado's most famous Fourteeners, the Maroon Bells, which top

Ashcroft was a silver boomtown between 1880 and 1883. When the Denver & Rio Grande Railroad did not extend its tracks beyond nearby Aspen in 1887, Ashcroft died.

False-fronted buildings in St. Elmo served miners from 1880 to the 1920s. An 1890 fire destroyed two blocks of the main street, including, disastrously, the town's liquor supply.

Opposite page: *Fabulous riches produced by Aspen silver mines are memorialized by many fine Victorian residences, such as this home occupied by clothier Jacob Sands in the 1890s.*

out at 14,156 feet in Maroon Bells–Snowmass Wilderness. The road to the wilderness portal at Maroon Lake is so jammed with admirers of the beautiful Bells that only buses are permitted from mid-July through Labor Day. These buses leave regularly from Aspen Highlands Ski Area.

Another extremely photogenic silver-mining area—but much harder to reach—is on the other side of the Bells from Maroon Lake. Silver mines in the Crystal River Valley boomed in the 1880s and were augmented by a quarry that produced very fine marble for such national shrines as the Lincoln Memorial and Tomb of the Unknown Soldier. Declining markets, transportation difficulties, and the propensity of the Crystal River to flood closed the quarries at Marble in 1941. Pure white blocks of marble deposited by floods are obvious in the Crystal River above Redstone, and marble also constitutes the world's fanciest riprap along the spur to Marble from Colorado Highway 133.

While the scenic beauty of the Crystal River Valley above Marble is hard to exaggerate, so is the miserable condition of the road. We have seen normal passenger cars travel as far as the much-photographed mill of the Lead King Mine perched above the river; we cannot testify, however, to the condition of those cars when (or if) they again reached pavement. A high-clearance vehicle is essential for driving above Marble. These can be rented in Marble, or you can take a commercial tour of the valley in an open-topped four-wheel-drive bus.

During the 1880s a well-traveled road extended out of the Crystal River Valley over Schofield Pass to the mining towns of Gothic and Crested Butte. This road today is definitely for four-wheel-drive enthusiasts. An easier alternative is Highway 133 over McClure Pass, then a left turn below Paonia Reservoir on a well-maintained, unpaved road over Kebler Pass. Climbing through magnificent aspen forests past outstanding views of West Elk Wilderness, this road passes the site of Irwin, an 1879 silver-mining camp.

Prospectors washed a million dollars' worth of placer gold from the streams around Crested Butte in the early 1860s, despite the dangers of Indians and avalanches. In 1877, coal deposits generated more interest in the area, and the Denver & Rio Grande pushed its narrow-gauge tracks into the fledgling town of Crested Butte in 1880. The town was a supply point for nearby mining camps, such as Irwin and Gothic, until the precious metals played out. From the late 1880s until 1952 more prosaic coal mining supported Crested Butte. Today the town maintains its Victorian mining-town look, while depending on tourists attracted to the ski slopes of Mount Crested Butte and the summer and fall beauties of Gunnison National Forest. However, valuable molybdenum lies beneath Mount Emmons, which towers over the town like an incipient avalanche of a new mining boom.

Gold seekers slipped by unfriendly Utes in 1871 to locate pay dirt amid such spectacular Fourteeners as Wetterhorn and Uncompahgre peaks. They returned in 1874 to start mining after the Utes gave up the land in the Brunot Treaty of 1873. After the fashion of the time, the rush of miners decreed their collection of shacks and a few substantial buildings to be a city—Lake City.

Lake City is best known for Alferd Packer, who killed, robbed, and ate all five of his mining companions in the winter of 1874. Hayden surveyors roaming by the following summer cheerfully named the site of his deed Cannibal Plateau. A marker just beyond the Lake Fork bridge on Colorado Highway 149 indicates where Alferd dined.

Packer was arrested for murder. He escaped and was recaptured nine years later. A Democratic judge berated the cannibal for eating most of Hinsdale County's Democrats and sentenced Packer to hang until he was "dead, dead, dead!" The county still votes Republican.

However, Packer escaped hanging because he had been arrested under the laws of Colorado Territory and tried under state law. Eventually, he served 15 years in jail for manslaughter. Today, Packer is memorialized by the student union cafeteria named in his honor at the University of Colorado. The Alferd Packer Feasting and Friendship Society based in Lake City is dedicated to

A dam just behind this Crystal River waterfall powered the rock-clinging mill that processed ore from the Lead King and other silver mines from the 1880s until 1916.

"Serving Our Fellow Man." The hottest-selling item in Lake City bookstores is an Alferd Packer cookbook.

Near Lake City is San Cristobal Lake, the second largest natural lake in Colorado. San Cristobal was dammed 700 years ago when the Slumgullion Earthflow blocked the Lake Fork of the Gunnison River. A huge mass of partially decomposed volcanic rock slumped four miles, from 11,500 feet on Cannibal Plateau to 8,800 feet at the lake. The earthflow is seen best from an overlook about five miles up Colorado Highway 149 from Lake City.

Following Colorado Highway 149 over Slumgullion

Pass brings you to Creede, once in the running as the wildest mining camp in Colorado. It boomed with the discovery of silver in its Holy Moses Mine in 1890 and busted in 1893 when the United States dropped its ruinous policy of subsidizing silver and began backing its currency only with gold. "It's day all day in the day time, and there is no night in Creede," wrote editor Cy Warman in the town's newspaper. This dubious claim of 24-hour hell-raisin' attracted surviving social misfits of the dying Old West: Bat Masterson, Calamity Jane, Poker Alice, and bunco artist "Soapy" Smith. Bob Ford—killer of Jesse James in St. Joseph, Missouri, a

decade earlier—was gunned down in his own saloon in Creede.

Changing times and technologies have seen revival of silver mining in Creede. But the shady entertainments of this mining camp have been replaced by performances of the Creede Repertory Theatre. Creede also has become a hiking and backpacking supply center, serving such hiker heavens as Weminuche and La Garita wilderness areas and Wheeler Geologic Area.

Mining continues also in Silverton, settled within weeks after the Utes gave up this dramatically lovely section of the San Juan Mountains in 1874. Supply center for one of the richest mining districts in the state, Silverton managed to survive the national switch to the gold standard in 1893 because the area produced much gold as well as silver.

Silverton also is the name of a narrow-gauge railroad that serves the town. One of the premier attractions in Colorado, the Silverton belches steam and smoke, and with a blast of its whistle, chugs out of Durango on a one-way journey to Silverton and back, just as it did a century ago. With the tracks set 3 feet apart rather than the standard gauge of 4 feet 8½ inches, the Silverton was able to climb steeper grades and round tighter curves.

Opposite page: William H. Jackson photographed Creede bustling with bonanza activity as it spilled from Willow Creek Canyon in 1891. From 1,000-foot volcanic monoliths echoed the racket of hammers, dynamite, honky-tonk pianos in 75 bars, and gunfire. It was quite a change from the 1874 serenity Jackson had recorded here for the Hayden Survey. Colorado Historical Society.
This page: A survey camp cook posed with Dutch oven biscuits for a 15-second exposure. With a dab of black paint on the negative, Jackson added the flying pancake. Colorado Historical Society.

Freight wagons hauled supplies to new mining camps and hauled out ore over toll roads scratched from difficult terrain. This type of transportation was arduous, hair-raising, and expensive. Only high-grade ore could justify such effort. Not until railroads laid serpentine routes that were less steep was it economically possible to tap much of Colorado's mineral wealth. Colorado Historical Society.

This adaptation for mountain railroading proves its advantage during the 44-mile trip. The train chugs its clackety-clack way through narrow rock cuts, creeps along a ledge blasted 400 feet above the churning Animas River, and traces the river's course through deep gorges in San Juan National Forest.

The yellow passenger cars are originals from 1878 or exact copies made in 1964. Many riders, however, opt for the better view of jagged 13,000-foot peaks available from open gondola cars at the rear of the train. Photographers include the steam engine and yellow passenger cars in pictures taken when the train is making one of its many tight curves. Those who choose the gondolas should be aware that mountain weather can turn cold any day of the year and that cinders rain down from the stack of the coal-fired locomotive.

A two-hour layover in Silverton affords time to roam along streets little changed over the last hundred years, during which hard-rock mining has remained an important element in the town's economy. The false-front buildings that housed infamous 24-hour-a-day pleasure palaces on Blair Street today contain tamer businesses oriented toward the hundreds of tourists who disembark from the Silverton daily in the summer. Reservations aboard this deservedly popular train should be made a month in advance.

Colorado's Rockies are America's most accessible high mountains because autos follow routes pioneered by railroads such as the Silverton, the sole mechanized transport along Animas Canyon.

The Denver & Rio Grande tracks twisted through 500 miles of mountain scenery to haul the wealth of Silverton mines to Denver. Another narrow-gauge section of that route still in operation begins at Antonito, the Colorado terminus of the Cumbres and Toltec Scenic Railway. This time machine carrying passengers back into the 1880s is owned by Colorado and New Mexico.

The train follows a coal-burning steam locomotive across the state line 11 times, traversing broad expanses of sagebrush, quivering aspen groves, and cliff-clinging rock shelves above Toltec Gorge. Train and history buffs board at mid-morning and ride to a lunch stop in the Colorado whistle stop of Osier. From Osier, you can ride back to Antonito or board another train to continue to Chama, New Mexico. From Chama, you are hauled along lovely State Highway 17 through Cumbres Pass back to Antonito. Both trains feature reasonably comfortable coaches and an open-to-the-elements-and-soot gondola car, generally jammed with photographers.

Photographers flock also to 1,200-foot-deep Royal Gorge, another point on the Denver & Rio Grande's route to the Rockies' riches. Across the gorge, now a Canon City park, have been flung the world's highest suspension bridge (1,055 feet) and an aerial tramway; an incline railway takes visitors down to the Arkansas River at the canyon bottom.

William J. Palmer's track layers pushed through this only practical rail route to the Leadville silver mines in an 1878–79 fight with the Atchison, Topeka, & Santa Fe. Employees of the rival railroads held opposite ends of the canyon, neither letting the other pass while the Royal Gorge War dragged on in the courts. Palmer's Denver & Rio Grande crews even threw up two small forts to defend their claims. Use of the right-of-way through the gorge finally was seized by General Palmer in a well-planned armed takeover of the line on June 11, 1879. In 1880, the two rail companies made peace and agreed how the southern Rockies would be divided between them.

Many Denver & Rio Grande routes through the San Juans were impossible; Otto Mears, one of Palmer's collaborators, built them anyway. Beginning with toll roads, Mears moved on to railroads and was directly responsible for much of the transportation that made possible the extraction of mineral wealth from these incredibly rugged volcanic peaks. At Bear Creek Falls, two miles south of Ouray, a plaque at the site of one of Mears's tollgates honors Colorado's pathfinder. Much of this toll route eventually became the Million Dollar Highway, one of the world's most spectacularly beautiful roads.

Miners on vacation from rich diggings to the south were fishing in the Ouray region when they discovered the Trout and Fisherman lodes in 1875. Soon the rush was on, and Ouray was laid out as a supply point for many mines in its vicinity. Silver was the main treasure until 1893, when the United States quit buying silver to back its currency. This disaster for many mining towns was offset in Ouray by the discovery of the Camp Bird Mine in 1896, which poured out $24 million in gold before 1902. It still is producing.

During its century of facing the ups and downs of mining economics that rival those of the local topography for suddenness, Ouray has learned the more refined techniques of a tourism industry. Natural hot springs in this volcanic country feed swimming pools in the town. Many jeeps are rented for touring through

unexcelled scenery on occasionally hair-raising roads, the legacy of the region's mining past.

Some of these roads, such as that over Ophir Pass, lead to Telluride. An easier way is Colorado Highway 62 along Otto Mears's route over extremely lovely Dallas Divide. Named for a metallic compound often associated with gold and silver ores, Telluride sometimes was pronounced "to hell you ride" when the town was a brawling mining camp in the 1870s and 1880s. In 1889, Butch Cassidy made an illegal withdrawal of $30,000 from the Telluride Bank. Otto Mears generated a big boom in 1890 when he pushed a railroad into town. Construction of the luxurious Sheridan Hotel in 1891 marked an increase in respectability, but not stability.

Telluride depended mostly on silver and fell on hard times in 1893, when America stopped subsidizing the price of silver. To a crowd of out-of-work miners in front of the Sheridan Hotel, 1896 presidential candidate William Jennings Bryan swore in resonant tones to absent Republicans, "You shall not press down upon the brow of labor this crown of thorns, you shall not crucify mankind upon a cross of gold." But since the alternative to crucifixion was economic ruin, the United States went on the gold standard, and Telluride went on the skids. When rich gold veins were discovered Telluride boomed again.

Now developed as a ski area, Telluride has preserved many of its 1890s Victorian buildings. Recreation is a thriving industry in summer and fall also, as silver creeks and aspen gold draw thousands of visitors to Telluride's spectacular amphitheater of 14,000-foot peaks in Uncompahgre National Forest.

Cripple Creek was the last and richest of Colorado's mining boomtowns. After the 1891 gold strike in this collapsed caldera of an ancient volcano, the population went from zero to 18,000 in less than two years. So vast was its wealth that Cripple Creek partially offset the economic devastation to Colorado caused by silver-mine closings in 1893. In fact, Cripple Creek mines dumped so much gold on international markets that its price fell, just as silver mines of Leadville and Aspen had driven

The world's highest suspension bridge spans Royal Gorge, cut through a hard wedge of granite, schist, and gneiss billions of years old extending from Pikes Peak.

Between 1880 and 1890, the route over Ophir Pass was a toll road, linking mills in Silverton with Ophir and Telluride until rails reached these rich mining districts.

down world prices. Ever higher production costs steadily eroded Cripple Creek gold mining until no gold was mined after 1962.

We remember walking as tourists through the streets of Cripple Creek in 1964, hearing old-timers comment longingly to each other that if the price of gold would rise just a little, the mines could reopen. Of course, the price of gold rose more than a little, and some Cripple Creek mines are producing again.

The Mollie Kathleen mine offers tours, and the Cripple Creek District Museum relates the history of this colorful town and the surrounding mines and communities. Most buildings in the town date from the brick construction era that began after a devastating fire in 1896.

During its height Cripple Creek was served by three railroads. The twisting routes of two of these now are exciting automobile roads. The Gold Camp Road winds past many old mines to Colorado Springs. The Phantom Canyon Road follows a deep and dramatic gorge from Victor down to Canon City. Both roads are unpaved but suitable for passenger cars in good weather.

Colorado mining towns—revived, converted, deserted, or disappeared—all testify to the optimism and energy generated by many people struggling to get filthy rich easily and immediately. The number that succeed, as everyone knows and knew, is tiny. Yet who of us wandering the bustling streets of Central City or the grassy ones of Ashcroft does not dream of making the big strike ourselves?

Sudden wealth is even more unlikely today than it was in the last half of the nineteenth century. Colorado holds no more undiscovered bonanzas. Improved extraction technology, though, has instigated more than one rush to the tailings piles and abandoned glory holes. Any of the mining districts we have described could boom again.

But no new technology and no capital investment are needed to extract the most valuable natural resource of Colorado. Unlimited spiritual riches are available to those who open their souls to extract all that is available from mountain beauty accented by the remnants of the mining era—the greatest treasure trove of the Rockies.

Much of the charm of Colorado's mining towns derives from their buildings. Above: The Imperial Hotel in Cripple Creek, decorated with an ad. Right: Restored homes in Telluride.

The Plains—Focus of Living

Vacationers heading for "Colorful Colorado" prefer to believe that the eastern third of the state does not exist. It is a perverse extension of Nebraska or Kansas, a barrier to be crossed on the way to the mountains. The state line, for these folks, runs north and south through Denver.

But, since the early days of the gold rushes, the bulk of Colorado's population has lived on the plains. Before 1859, Indian tribes waged vicious wars against each other in order to live on the plains instead of in the mountains. Nice as they are to look at, the mountains offer few ways to make a living, and their weather is somewhat trying. It is said that there are only two seasons in the mountains: winter and the Fourth of July.

Zebulon Pike in his 1810 report of his exploration of Colorado told of a desert east of the Rockies. In *Account of an Expedition from Pittsburgh to the Rocky Mountains*, Edwin James reported that Stephen Long's 1820 exploration crossed a dreary plain, "almost wholly unfit for cultivation, and of course uninhabitable by a people depending on agriculture for their subsistence." James's map of the area labels the country between mid-Kansas and the Rockies as the Great Desert. Subsequent explorers made essentially the same observation, and the concept of the Great American Desert held back settlement of the plains for a generation.

Since 1859 Colorado boosters either have taken offense at this statement or chuckled about it. How, they ask, could a desert have supported the "wild game, incalculable numbers of which find ample pasture and subsistence upon it," as James also reported in his *Account*? Today, agriculture on the Great American Desert is one of Colorado's main industries.

However, the reports of Pike, Long, and the other explorers were dead accurate, except for misinterpretation of one word: desert. To many people living in the humid East, desert meant Sahara-like drifting sand. Eastern Colorado does, in fact, have some sand dunes. And the Colorado plains share a very dry climate with the rest of the Great Plains west of the 100th meridian that runs through mid-Nebraska and Kansas. East of this approximate boundary, where average annual precipitation is 20 inches or more, unirrigated agriculture is reasonably workable.

The average precipitation is 14 inches in eastern Colorado, but averages do not tell the whole story. All over the plains periodic droughts occur, with precipitation falling far below average. Similarly, there are wet cycles when precipitation is significantly above average. These fluctuations are certain, but their intensity, duration, geographic range, and the number of years between them are unpredictable.

Aridity on the plains is made worse by wind, which sweeps across the open landscape with little to slow it down. Particularly hot, dry winds from the south greatly increase evaporation of the little moisture there is. Windbreaks, trees of various species planted in ranks, shield older houses and other buildings on the plains; it takes many years for carefully nurtured trees to grow to a useful height. Each one of them is precious beyond thought.

Occasionally, you will see trees where houses once stood. The trees mark the graves of hopes buried by drought and wind.

In 1859, the mining boom demanded a local source of food. The plains were sufficiently warm and, as sellers of agricultural real estate always pointed out, very fertile. Produce gardens soon were growing along irrigation ditches scratched in the bottomlands along the South Platte.

The obvious need was to irrigate outside the narrow bottoms with mountain water from slowly melting snow. But one farmer could not raise enough money to build miles-long irrigation ditches. Irrigation dictated

Symbol of the plains, a windmill pumps well water that is stored in a tank. Stock tanks quench the thirsts of deer and pronghorn as well as cattle and horses.

cooperative rather than independent farming, and so agricultural colonies were born.

An idealistic agricultural reporter for Horace Greeley's *New York Tribune*, Nathan Meeker, organized more than 200 like-minded Easterners to follow the *Tribune*'s advice and go west. They founded Union Colony in 1870 on prime land along the Cache la Poudre River. The colony built the irrigation ditches and laid out a town in lots where the members would live. Each member got 160 acres of land and a lot in town. The town was named Greeley to honor the publisher of the *Tribune*.

Greeley's population soon grew to 1,500, with some 400 homes and many substantial public buildings. This thumping success soon was imitated by other colonies up and down the Front Range at such places as Longmont and Fort Collins. Today, the colony organization has been supplanted by water corporations and irrigation districts. Irrigated crops include corn, alfalfa, sugar beets, and a wide variety of fruits and vegetables.

Where no water is available from mountain runoff, deep wells have been sunk. Many of these wells tap water imprisoned in rock layers far below the surface, water that has not seen the sun since the glaciers melted. Today, giant center-pivot sprinkler systems irrigate half-mile-wide green circles on the plains, demolishing even the centuries-old notion that fields should be rectangular. But this ice-age water is not being replaced as fast as it is being pumped. At the present rate of use, 25 percent of this water will be gone by the year 2020. When groundwater is gone or requires more energy to pump than the crops it grows are worth, irrigation on the fields it waters will stop, just as mining stops when ore is used up or extraction costs are too high.

On those fields where irrigation is impractical, the temptation always exists to try dry farming, especially in wet years. But the droughts always come; they are normal. Historically, each generation of dry-land farmers has suffered economic disaster that drives many off the land, only to be replaced by others who try dry farming again. This pattern repeated itself through droughts of the 1890s, 1930s, and 1950s, punctuated by less serious

At the Garden of the Gods, a Colorado Springs park, the white sandstone hogback dates from 135 million years ago, more than 100 million years younger than the red sandstone.

Left: *Oil wells pump black gold from pools in Dakota sandstone of the Denver Basin, nearly a mile below the plains.*

Below: *At the 400-acre Monfort feedlot near Greeley, cattle that have grown to between 675 and 850 pounds grazing on the plains are fed cornflakes and alfalfa for 100 to 150 days until they reach the slaughtering weight of 1,150 pounds. Each day 750 tons of grain are processed at this feedlot to feed 100,000 cattle.*

droughts among the major ones. Even worse than individual disasters has been the cumulative degradation of the plains through loss of soil in devastating dust storms.

From the ruin of infamous dust bowls of the 1930s grew the national grasslands in Colorado—Pawnee in the north, Comanche in the south. Patched together from abused land that no longer was economically useful, the national grasslands have been restored by the U.S. Forest Service to approach their former productivity. Key to any good land management in the arid, unforgiving western U.S. is a bias toward long-term health of the land instead of realization of immediate benefits. Thus, some lands should be kept in pasture instead of being plowed. Livestock on pasture lands should be few enough so that grass can grow back as fast as they eat it.

Native grasses adapted to drought, such as gramma and buffalo grass, are low-growing with shallow roots that form sod. They grow quickly after spring rains and then become dormant brown. Such grasses form a tasty and nutritious forage for cattle, as they did for millions of bison before buffalo herds were wiped out in the 1870s. Although bison no longer roam the national grasslands, the deer and the antelope still play. Also present are smaller wild animals: prairie dogs, coyotes, golden eagles, and many other birds, including the lark bunting, state bird of Colorado, which is rarely seen in the mountains.

On private lands, soil-conservation districts encourage strip-cropping to protect plowed land from wind erosion. Grains, primarily wheat, are grown in strips that alternate with strips of stubble to hold soil and collect moisture. Windmills, omnipresent symbol of the plains, pump wells dug in a dispersed pattern to spread out the wear and tear of grazing. The U.S. Soil Conservation Service helps ranchers rotate their stock to give pastures periodic rest.

Unlike the cooperation required by irrigation, cattle ranching in Colorado developed along the lines of extreme independence, huge ranches resembling self-contained feudal estates. In the 1860s and 1870s John Wesley Iliff created a domain of Texas longhorns next to the town of Greeley, which today still boasts the world's largest cattle feedlot. Iliff and his fellow cattle barons obtained key 160-acre plots along streams by having cowboys or whoever wandered by file on the land under the terms of the Homestead Act of 1862. Never intending to really settle the land, these bogus homesteaders then sold the titles to the ranchers for a pittance. This fraud was standard operating procedure in the West, in large part because the Homestead Act itself was completely impractical, based on eastern farming techniques. Once they owned the watered lands, cattlemen controlled all the surrounding federal grasslands, which were useless without water.

Fattening cattle for two years on free grass was enormously profitable. Iliff shrewdly increased his profits by selective breeding of his longhorns with high-quality eastern bulls. These upgraded cattle sold well to feed the miners, railroad builders, and army in the 1860s and 1870s. He had many imitators, especially among foreign investors, who by 1875 were fattening half a million cattle on federal land.

The inspiration of the cowboy, most popular of American folk heroes, these ranching empires fell as quickly as they had sprouted. They used up the cheap longhorns from Texas, which eventually were barred from Colorado as disease carriers. Other cattle produced better beef but had a lower survival rate on the Colorado plains. Cattle raisers overgrazed the land and suffered competition from sheepmen, whom the cattlemen ironically accused of killing off the grass. Overgrazing was worsened by drought. Particularly bad winters wiped out large herds.

But the crushing blow was barbed wire, invented in 1874. Barbed wire held even longhorns at bay. Its use spread quickly and ended the open range on which cattle empires were based. Today cattle ranches are fenced more rigorously than any other land, much to the disappointment of Easterners who come to Colorado expecting wide open spaces in the domain of the cowboy.

Proper farming and ranching practices rapidly are becoming irrelevant along the base of the Front Range, where cities sprawl across once rural scenes. The mountains and their recreational resources are attracting throngs of new residents in a population explosion that makes past mining booms seem very minor by comparison. Land-use decisions already have been made that decree an eventually continuous city with few rural breaks between Fort Collins and Colorado Springs. Water, it is said in Colorado, runs uphill toward money; farmers cannot afford to bid as high for the available water as metropolitan users can. And land used for agricultural purposes cannot generate a tiny fraction of the profits that the same land will generate when used for urban purposes.

Denver is Colorado's capital, largest city, and the hub from which most economic activity in the Rocky Mountains radiates. Denver City began in 1859 as a collection of various towns to serve miners flocking to newly discovered gold fields along Cherry and Clear creeks. Consolidation of the towns and incorporation of Denver came in 1861.

Most opinion holds that the city's name honors Gen. James W. Denver, the 1859 governor of Kansas Territory, which contained part of Colorado. A minority view claims that an army colonel riding by when a group of land speculators was laying out the town predicted that the new village never would amount to much. With typical Western irony, the developers named their new town for skeptical Colonel Denver.

To first-time Colorado visitors pursuing dreams of Rocky Mountain highs, Denver can be disappointing. It is a big city set on the flat plains, much like any other except that its western horizon is the spectacular Front Range. For folks eager to reach the mountains, Denver is one last obstacle to get past as quickly as possible.

This first impression is unfortunate. While Denver is not an idyllic wilderness, it offers both residents and visitors more than most cities can boast. The Denver Museum of Natural History in City Park contains one of the world's finest collections of North American Indian artifacts, and its life-size dioramas of worldwide wildlife habitats are outstanding. The excellent Denver Zoo also is in City Park, and Denver Botanic Gardens are just a short drive away. An interesting contrast between historic residences is the 1859 log-cabin simplicity of Four Mile House (the oldest house in Denver) and the Molly Brown House, 1889 Victorian mansion of a legendary Colorado heroine.

Denver's downtown skyline seems to change daily as glittering glass towers supply offices for energy and financial corporations. Two recent additions of special interest are the Denver Art Museum and the Denver Center for the Performing Arts, with its marvelous theaters and concert halls. But even in glittering new Denver, the past has its place in Larimer Square, a cluster of shops and restaurants that gains charm and popularity from its restoration of 1880s buildings. Although dwarfed by surrounding skyscrapers, the Colorado Capitol, set atop a hill with its gold dome shining in the sun, continues to dominate the downtown area. During football season, winning or losing, the Denver Broncos dominate the entire city, firmly in the grip of orange-tinted Bronco Mania.

Because the ranch and farm land between Denver and Boulder is filling rapidly with urban sprawl, the two cities and their suburbs often are thought of as simply the Denver-Boulder area. Boulder, home of the University of Colorado, is dominated by uplifted sedimentary slabs called the Flatirons. These are included in 5,280 acres of municipal parklands. Flagstaff Scenic Highway snakes its way to the top of Flagstaff Mountain 1,600 feet above Boulder. Established in 1858 as a farming and gold-mining center, Boulder now is home to leading scientific institutions and high technology industries.

The second center of population along the Front Range is Colorado Springs. It was founded in 1871 by railroad tycoon William J. Palmer specifically to serve people who came to the state to appreciate beautiful mountains. There were no springs at Colorado Springs. But many fashionable resorts in the East were springs, and so the word was included in the name of Colorado's first big-time resort. Manitou Springs do bubble up nearby, naturally carbonated by passing through limestone and therefore presumably healthful. Water dissolving limestone has formed Cave of the Winds, the state's only commercially developed limestone cave.

Sufferers from respiratory disorders (the "one-lung brigade") also flocked to Colorado Springs to benefit from clear, clean, invigorating mountain air. In 1881, Palmer's Denver & Rio Grande Railroad published a booklet, *Health, Wealth, and Pleasure in Colorado and New Mexico*, to encourage health-seekers to tour and settle in Colorado. The dream of unpolluted air and water (unfortunately not as pristine as in the 1870s) and life in the great outdoors still draws new residents. But they seek a healthy life-style rather than a magic-atmosphere fix for a vague pulmonary disorder.

Above: Denver's skyline is constantly changing as new towers rise to house the business activity of this economic hub of the Rocky Mountain West.

Right: The state capitol with its Corinthian architecture of Colorado granite and gold leaf–covered dome, built between 1887 and 1895, still dominates the city's center.

The Flatirons above the University of Colorado, in Boulder, were formed by the erosion of the ancestral Rockies, which were then set on edge by the rise of the modern Rockies.

Set at the foot of famous Pikes Peak and near the eroded, red sandstone sculpture of Garden of the Gods, the Springs (as it often is abbreviated today) never disappointed seekers of scenery. One of these was Katharine Lee Bates, who traveled in 1893 on a carriage road to the top of Pikes Peak and was inspired to write "O beautiful for spacious skies,/For amber waves of grain,/For purple mountain majesties/Above the fruited plain!", the opening lines of "America the Beautiful," the nation's favorite patriotic hymn.

The most popular attraction of Colorado Springs today is man-made. The design of the U.S. Air Force Academy chapel with its sharply angled spires is reminiscent of Colorado topography, which may be why the chapel is touted as the second most popular tourist attraction in the state. (The first is Rocky Mountain National Park, a chapel in its own right.) A self-guided auto tour circles through the campus.

Pueblo is the population center of southern Colorado. Built on the Arkansas River, it too was significantly influenced by William Palmer, who began steel production in Pueblo. Today CF & I Steel Corporation operates one of the largest steel plants located west of Chicago.

East along the Arkansas River, near the melon fields of Rocky Ford and La Junta, is Bent's Old Fort National Historic Site. National Park Service archaeologists have reconstructed the old fort in meticulous detail. The Park

Service owns sufficient surrounding land to exclude modern distractions. Glittering automobiles are restricted to a parking lot several hundred yards away; electric carts provide transportation for those unable to walk to the fort. Park Service staff are costumed in frontier dress accurate to the smallest detail. Bent's Old Fort is one of the world's finest living-history projects. Kit Carson and the other mountain men who frequented the fort in the 1830s and 1840s would feel at home there today.

It seems significant that Bent's Old Fort, set far out on the plains with the mountains visible only dimly if at all, was the first semipermanent settlement of whites in Colorado. From then until now, the focus of attention has been on the mountains. But the focus of living has been on the plains.

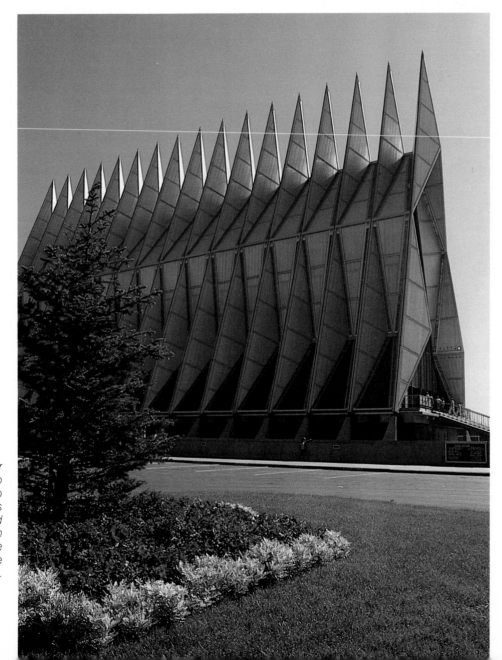

The cadet chapel at the U.S. Air Force Academy near Colorado Springs contains separate worship centers to serve the spiritual needs of Protestant, Roman Catholic, and Jewish cadets. Its 17 aluminum spires lead eye and mind to the wide, blue sky where cadets are destined to serve their nation.

Canyon Country

Disaster struck at noon, June 7, 1869. Running four boats down a canyon they had just named Lodore, the explorers of the Colorado River led by John Wesley Powell hit a major rapid. The one-armed Major Powell, scouting ahead in the *Emma Dean*, directed his boat ashore, then signaled the others to follow. The men in the *No-Name* missed the signal.

Too late they realized their peril. An irresistible avalanche of water swept the *No-Name* into the rapids. Its crew of three managed the first fall, but then all were thrown into the roaring water when the boat crashed against a boulder. They desperately hauled themselves back into the *No-Name*, now full of water and kept afloat only by her watertight compartments. Completely out of control, the boat was tossed through the first rapid and rushed into a second, 200 yards further on. There she crashed broadside into a boulder and broke in half.

Miraculously, the three boatmen survived and eventually were pulled to safety. But the loss of the *No-Name* and the supplies she carried haunted the expedition. The discouragement caused largely by this loss manifested itself the following August 28 in the Grand Canyon. Two of the *No-Name's* boatmen plus another explorer abandoned Powell's expedition in the Grand Canyon. Giving up on the brink of success, they scaled the canyon walls to reach civilization overland. Their bodies were later found, full of Indian arrows.

Canyon of Lodore is cut by the Colorado River's main tributary, the Green River, where it loops through the northwest corner of Colorado. Here in Dinosaur National Monument the Yampa River joins the Green in Echo Park, named by the Powell expedition as they shouted their joy after escaping from Lodore. The national monument originally included only the dinosaur fossil quarries across the state line in Utah. Later Dinosaur was expanded to include magnificent canyon scenery carved by the Green and Yampa rivers. Playground of white-water boating enthusiasts in the mold of Powell, this wilderness maze is seen most easily from a scenic road leading to a short trail to Harpers Corner.

The Colorado River and its tributaries have carved all the plateau region of western Colorado. Two other national monuments and a national park protect some of the most interesting or spectacular canyons. Innumerable other gorges complete a colorful maze of bare rock that makes up Colorado's canyon country.

Not as deep or steep as the canyons of the Yampa and Green, the valley of the White River is green with irrigated pasture contrasting with stark, bare cliffs above. Powell Park, a particularly lovely meadow, is named for the major who camped there before his journey down the Green and Colorado. In Powell Park, Nathan Meeker established a new agency headquarters for the Utes in 1878, near the town named Meeker today. The idealistic founder of Union Colony at Greeley had been fired from his administrative position by colonists whom he had begun to irritate after nine years. Some disliked his hostility toward alcoholic beverages; others thought him an atheist; still others disliked his defense of publisher William Byers during an adultery scandal.

Greeley was a very successful farming colony, and such diverse criticism perhaps indicated that Meeker was behaving fairly and evenhandedly. But at age 60 he was out of a job, deeply in debt, and even more deeply discouraged. Then he was offered the job of Indian agent for the Utes. Meeker could be trusted to be honest in a position that sometimes had been filled with political appointees inclined to steal federal funds earmarked for the Indians.

Meeker undertook his new job with wholehearted enthusiasm not particularly tempered by wisdom. Sincerely trying to help the Utes adjust to white civilization, Meeker succeeded only in alienating them. In September, 1879, they massacred Meeker and various other whites within reach.

Black Canyon of the Gunnison National Monument contains the narrowest and deepest canyon in the United States: 2,425 feet deep and 1,300 feet wide.

Fields of the Grand Valley below the austere Book Cliffs are irrigated by the Colorado River, called the Grand River before 1921. The Grand joined the Green River in Utah to form the Colorado. Utah's legislature planned to rename the Green the Colorado. Irritated legislators in Denver beat the Utahans to the punch and changed the Grand River to the Colorado, which now originates in Rocky Mountain National Park and flows across half the state.

A hiker atop cliffs of Weber sandstone at Harpers Corner in Dinosaur National Monument watches the Green River cut through rocks upturned by the Mitten Park fault.

The Coke Ovens in Colorado National Monument. Lines across the walls mark dunes that are 200 million years old.

This was not entirely bad news to whites who had coveted Ute land for years. In short order, northern bands of Utes directly connected with the Meeker massacre were banished to Utah deserts. Southern bands were confined to a less grim reservation in the southern part of Colorado.

Lovely, forested highlands were thereby opened to settlement. They are crossed today by roads over the White River and Uncompahgre plateaus, Douglas Pass, and the switchbacks of Grand Mesa. Ute campfires were barely cold before orchardists began planting fruit trees north and west of Grand Mesa around Paonia and Grand Junction.

Also available were the energy resources of coal pointed out in 1877 by the Hayden Survey's *Atlas of Colorado*. To be exploited later were uranium and oil deposits. Maybe most valuable of all were oil-shale layers in the Piceance Basin bounded by Parachute and Rifle, where means of processing oil shale are being investigated today.

But it is canyons that dominate most people's impression of the plateau country. Colorado National Monument, a short way off Interstate 70 near Grand Junction, is a 20,445-acre maze of sheer-walled, thousand-foot-deep canyons accented with monolithic monuments. Rim Rock Drive passes many spectacular features on its 22-mile serpentine path between the east and west entrances. Numerous scenic turnouts, such as Cold Shivers Point, provide grand opportunities to appreciate sculpture carved by natural forces of erosion in colorful sedimentary rock. In the distance are green and gold irrigated fields along the Colorado River, and the Book Cliffs resemble a moonscape along the oil shale–rich Roan Plateau. Several self-guided nature trails, as well as longer trails, begin on Rim Rock Drive. On the latter, hikers should be sure to carry an adequate supply of water in this very arid plateau country.

Black Canyon of the Gunnison National Monument contains 12 miles of the extraordinarily deep and narrow gorge of the Gunnison River. Most often visited is the south rim, easily accessible from Montrose. The comparatively deserted north rim is 14 unpaved miles from Crawford. Views are equally spectacular from roads along both rims, which sometimes are closer to each other (1,300 feet at the Narrows) than to the river 1,730 to 2,425 feet below.

In typical Western fashion, such extravagantly dramatic scenery inspired even more extravagant exaggeration. For instance, the name of the gorge derived from its extreme depth and narrowness, which shut out the sun's light from the canyon bottom. So dark was the canyon floor that artful prevaricators claimed that when standing down there at noon they could see stars. A few gullible folks might well believe this yarn, for it is a very arduous climb into and back out of the canyon to check the veracity of the tales. The canyon's deep shadows and steep narrow walls formed because it is cut through extremely hard gneiss, which will support such steep walls without eroding to a more gradual pitch.

Part of the Black Canyon of the Gunnison contains reservoirs backed up in Curecanti National Recreation Area. There are three reservoirs in the recreation area—Blue Mesa, Morrow Point, and Crystal, all part of the Colorado River Storage Project. Colorado Highway 92, which cuts in and out of Curecanti, offers many fine views, especially of the rock pillar called Curecanti's Needle.

The streams of the Mancos River have sliced deeply into Mesa Verde, creating canyons that contain the national park's cliff dwellings. The top of the "green table" is a magical place suspended 2,000 feet above the Mancos River Valley and separated from the outside world by 21 miles of twisting mountain road. Chapin Mesa Museum sits on a canyon rim, overlooking Spruce Tree House, the best preserved of the large cliff dwellings in the national park. It contains 114 rooms and probably housed between 100 and 150 people. The ruin was named for Douglas firs growing nearby, a species that once was called Douglas spruce. Botanists changed the tree name; archaeologists kept the ruin name the same.

Nearby are hundreds of other ruins, including Square Tower House, Sun Temple, Balcony House, and Cliff Palace. Entering any cliff dwelling without a ranger present to protect the ruin is strictly forbidden, as is removal of any artifact. During the summer, a 12-mile bus ride leads to other ruins on Wetherill Mesa. The road is closed to private vehicles, and ruins at Wetherill continue to be excavated and readied for public visits.

Visitors who enter ruins at Mesa Verde will find the ruins stabilized but not restored. Stabilization involves replacing fallen rocks into walls with a masonry visually similar to the original. Some ruin walls also are "capped" with mortarlike concrete. Steel reinforcing rods may be hidden within a structure. Access to the ruins often is via very sturdy ladders that imitate cliff-dweller styles.

The result is a very neat, almost antiseptic, ruin. The artificialness of stabilization is essential, however, if visitors are to be permitted to enter *kivas* (subterranean worship centers), view the world from a cliff dweller's perspective, and enjoy poking around. Stabilization not only halts further natural erosion of the ruins; it cuts down on the erosion by thousands of clambering feet. And stabilization also protects visitors from being crushed under a collapsing stone wall or tripping over a loose rock.

Hovenweep National Monument is a collection of six Anasazi Indian sites that extends into Utah. Constructed by the same culture that built Mesa Verde's cliff dwellings, Hovenweep is much less visited than its famous cousin. Its isolation is due in large measure to its accessibility only by unpaved roads.

At the edge of the Colorado River where it first cuts into the plateau country, generations of Ute Indians soothed their aching muscles in Yampa Hot Springs. In

Cliff Palace, largest ruin in Mesa Verde National Park, was a 200-room apartment house seven centuries ago, sheltering 300 to 400 people under a huge protecting ledge of sandstone.

the Gay Nineties, silver-mining entrepreneur Walter Devereux diverted the Colorado to expose the springs and developed them into a spa. Today Glenwood Springs boasts the largest outdoor mineral hot springs pool in the world. Stretching out for 405 feet, it stays at 85 to 90 degrees Fahrenheit through mixing of cold surface water and waters from the hot springs, which are between 124 and 130 degrees. In 1893, the Hotel Colorado was built next to the pool, copying Italian architecture at the cost of $850,000. Such an opulent structure attracted the social elite of the world, including Presidents Theodore Roosevelt and William Howard Taft.

East of Glenwood Springs is Glenwood Canyon, a narrow 17-mile gorge cut by the Colorado River. The Colorado carries much silt, which acts as a rasp or sandpaper, grinding the canyon still deeper below its castellated walls.

North of Glenwood, and totally unrelated to Yampa Hot Springs, the Yampa River flows into the plateau country at Steamboat Springs. Steamboat was named for a hot spring that noisily emitted spray reminiscent of a riverboat's exhaust. Although the spring no longer exists, about 150 others in the vicinity contain a wide variety of minerals. Some of these feed into spas much frequented by skiers sore and weary from a day on the slopes or ski touring through the woods of Routt National Forest. Steamboat also attracts many visitors to its summer beauties, including flower-filled meadows of nearby Rabbit Ears Pass.

Perhaps the greatest attractions of plateau country are lonesome canyons undistinguished by a park, a sign, or even a name. In these wild places, modern visitors may approach the exhilaration that came to Powell and other early explorers. Still largely empty, the canyon country offers you a sense of being the first person to tread these rocks since the Indians left. But to those who do not pay attention or who permit themselves even a moment of carelessness, the rivers, canyons, and plateaus can be just as dangerous as they were to the crew of the *No-Name*.

Rocky Mountain Wild

Unfortunately, F. O. Stanley had only three months to live, said his doctor. But this time might be extended a bit if the highly successful inventor of the Stanley Steamer and various other lucrative devices would slow down and retreat to the healthful climate of Colorado. Therefore, in 1903, from the railhead in Lyons, Stanley set out on a trip that some people thought likely to cut short his life immediately. He drove one of his own motorcars along the wagon road to Estes Park Village below Longs Peak.

Before Stanley pioneered the motorcar, most tourism in the Rockies was on narrow-gauge railroads that had been built to haul ore from the mines. These trains twisted through mountains that were more than adequately spectacular, and the railroads quickly realized extra profits by hauling tourists. Since very little mineral wealth was mined around Longs Peak, no train was built to Estes Park. Ironically, this magical scenery close to population centers was harder to reach than remote scenery around Aspen or Silverton.

Stanley changed that situation in 1907 when he bought extensive real estate in Estes Park and completed a good road for his steamers from Lyons. In 1909 the Stanley Hotel opened. Stanley also led the way in such community development activities as an electricity-generating plant, sewage and water systems, and importing of Yellowstone elk to replace those wiped out by market hunting. The inventor lived another 37 years after his doctor's mistaken diagnosis.

Stanley had worked with his twin brother in inventing their famous steamer. Together they made another significant contribution to Colorado tourism in 1904. They sold to Eastman Kodak the patent to a dry photographic plate machine that they had invented in 1886. This technology made photography much easier, putting it within the abilities of an amateur. So much Kodak film is exposed in Colorado today that the little yellow boxes might appropriately be displayed on the state flag.

F. O. Stanley also allied himself with another Estes Park innkeeper, author and naturalist Enos Mills, in the effort to preserve the scenery around Estes Park within a national park. Success came in 1915 with the establishment of Rocky Mountain National Park.

The motorcar revolution and the preservation of convenient, remarkable scenery in Rocky Mountain National Park brought people flocking to Estes Park, which eventually became the most popular goal for visitors to the mountains. Today about 3 million people a year visit the national park, most during the summer. Nearly all arrive in the mechanical descendants of Stanley Steamers, although several hundred thousand leave their cars to walk the trails.

Rocky Mountain National Park and the wilderness areas in Colorado national forests are the habitat of the hiker and backpacker, and to a lesser degree the horse or llama packer. Rocky Mountain wilds are the core of Colorado's image, even for those much more likely to buy a six-pack than a backpack. Untamed land molds the Colorado mood, setting the tone for the state's informal but intense attitudes, customs, and life-styles.

Of course, most people experience untamed Colorado from roads along wilderness thresholds. This certainly is the quickest and most convenient way to penetrate the mountains. Even though it lacks the intensity and depth of nonmotorized travel, traveling by car provides worthwhile experiences if passengers are sensitive to the marvelous diversity that is passing by outside their windows.

For instance, to drive from Denver to the top of Trail Ridge Road in Rocky Mountain National Park is the ecological equivalent of driving thousands of miles north to the Arctic Circle. Each thousand feet of altitude gained takes mountain visitors through the same kinds of plant

A cross-country skier at the head of Odessa Gorge admires the craggy cliffs of Notchtop Mountain, carved by glaciers in Rocky Mountain National Park.

zones that they would encounter by traveling 600 miles to the north.

From mile-high Denver, you travel through the land of buffalo grass and plains cottonwood to penetrate the upturned strata of sedimentary rocks that would be named mountains anywhere else. Here they are lumped together as foothills and clothed with Rocky Mountain junipers (sometimes called cedars) and stubby ponderosa pines.

Scattered among the few open areas that remain along the base of the foothills are a few prairie-dog towns, now under siege and soon to be wiped out by land development. Mule deer appear to be holding their own for now among the foothills suburbs. You are virtually certain to see long-tailed, iridescent black-and-white birds that never fail to excite visitors to the West. These are magpies, looking for a roadside meal of squashed prairie dog or thirteen-lined ground squirrel.

The ponderosas become more ponderous as you begin to drive up river-cut canyons, gateways to the high country. Climbing beyond sedimentary rocks, the highways soon are threading through steep-walled defiles of obdurate schist, gneiss, and granite. Cottonwoods still grow at streamside, but the narrow-leafed species begins to mix with the plains cottonwood. Willows, alders, and water birches form brush thickets that provide superb habitat for a wide variety of animals ranging from mule deer to tiny yellow warblers.

Observant motorists begin to notice that the trees on one side of the road look different from the trees on the other side. Exposed to more direct sunlight, south-facing slopes are drier than those that face north, where soil is not baked constantly by the sun. Different plants have adapted to grow in soils of different moisture contents.

This difference is particularly easy to see in Colorado, where tree species are less diverse and easier to recognize than in deciduous forests of the East. On sunny south slopes you may see grass, brush, and prickly pear cactus growing opposite ponderosas on north slopes. As you climb higher into slightly less arid country, widely spaced ponderosas may take over south slopes across the valley from closely packed Douglas firs. This natural difference may be altered by the quaking aspen groves that grew here after the conifers were removed either by

fire or for lumber to fuel mining booms. These groves are the favored spots of pilgrims seeking aspen gold in autumn.

After climbing above 8,000 feet you have to descend to enter Estes Park, formed when a fault block dropped during the last major uplift of the Rockies 5 to 7 million years ago. The horseshoe bends of the Big Thompson River, among which Joel Estes settled in 1860, are drowned beneath Lake Estes, completed in 1948 for hydroelectric and irrigation purposes. Lake Estes is a link in Colorado's most ambitious diversion of Colorado River water to the eastern slope.

So magnificent are snow-accented peaks rising above Estes Park that many visitors fail to notice the rounded granite domes of Lumpy Ridge to the north. Though prosaically named, Lumpy Ridge is poetically lovely. Within Rocky Mountain National Park, it is the unspoiled backdrop for what may be the most beautifully situated cattle ranch in the world. MacGregor Ranch dates from 1874. Never a particularly profitable operation so high in the mountains, MacGregor Ranch is kept running by a cadre of dedicated volunteers who labor against great obstacles to maintain its historic operation. Visitors are welcome, but most folks overlook this gem tucked below Lumpy Ridge.

Those who do not need goods or services provided in Estes Park Village can bypass the town near the white Stanley Hotel and proceed directly to Rocky Mountain National Park. At 8,242 feet above sea level, the park's Fall River entrance is in the montane zone of vegetation, which extends from 6,000 to 9,000 feet. Here ponderosas grow widely spaced, and wildflower color explodes after a snowy spring. Aspens line the river, the rustle of their quaking leaves accompanying the music of falling water. The entrance station is a likely place to see mule deer and the descendants of Stanley's Yellowstone elk.

Deer and elk frequent this area because it provides the three basic needs that all animals require in their habitat: food, water, and shelter. They can drink from Fall River, take shelter in the woods, and eat in the meadow alongside the road. This area is especially valuable as winter range for the elk, for there is relatively little habitat available to them in winter within the national park.

Most elk used to migrate in winter all the way down

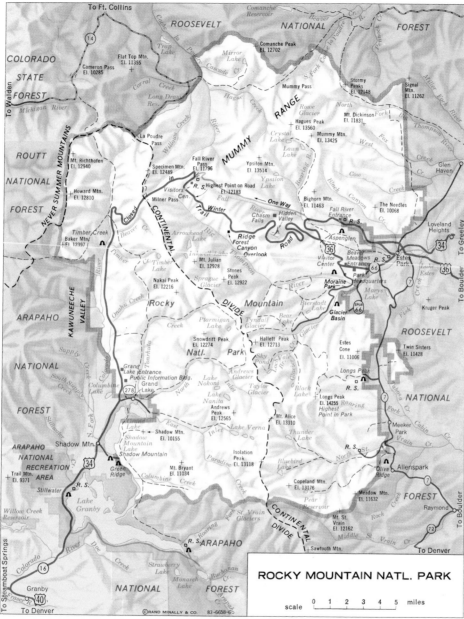

ROCKY MOUNTAIN NATL. PARK

scale 0 1 2 3 4 5 miles

©RAND McNALLY & CO.   83-6658-60

Rocky Mountain National Park encompasses 266,957 acres of broad, steep-sided valleys more than 8,000 feet above sea level and 107 peaks rising above 12,000 feet. All are dominated by the 14,255-foot majesty of Longs Peak. Between the gateway villages of Estes Park and Grand Lake winds Trail Ridge Road, four miles of which traverse alpine ridges more than 12,000 feet in altitude.

to the plains. Expanding human population long ago bottled them up in the mountains, where there is less for them to eat in winter than at lower elevations. As human settlement laps ever higher up the canyons, elk winter habitat decreases proportionately. The herds are pushed higher into the mountains, where fewer of them can survive winter's rigors.

Since hunting is not permitted in Rocky Mountain National Park, animals here tend to revert to their natural, unconcerned attitude toward people. This lack of fear makes wildlife easier to see. But the greatest service national parks provide for animals is not safety from hunters but preservation of habitat.

Keeping the land in a condition to support wildlife is really more important than protecting individual animals. Replacing willow thickets with condominiums destroys flocks of multihued warblers by removing their nesting habitat. Cutting down dead trees for firewood eliminates nest sites for chickadees, bluebirds, and a host of other hole-nesting animals. Chain saws and bulldozers ultimately are more deadly than shotguns and rifles.

There is a myth abroad in the land that when an animal's home is destroyed it can move someplace else. But "someplace else" does not exist. All wildlife habitats, including national parks and forests, automatically fill to capacity. When humans supplant wild animals, those animals either die or supplant other animals, which die. The only alternative is artificially providing food, shelter, and water when those necessities are removed.

Beyond the park entrance, the road climbs over a terminal moraine to Horseshoe Park, a large meadow favored by elk in winter and bighorn sheep in early summer. Thus, it is a favorite haunt of park visitors all the time. Signs in Horseshoe Park serve notice that visitors should not harass mountain sheep by trying to approach them closely for photographs. Either use a very long telephoto lens or resign yourself to just looking.

This policy, enforced by the presence of park rangers in summer, allows the sheep to eat mud at mineral licks in Horseshoe Park. The licks provide elements essential

In Bighorn Flats in Rocky Mountain National Park, a backpacker enjoys marsh marigolds and Parry primroses in unglaciated alpine tundra 12,000 feet above sea level.

for good health. Protecting bighorn access to vital minerals in the mud permits more visitors to see the sheep by cutting down natural mortality, increasing the size of the park herd. The policy also prevents one enthusiastic photographer from chasing off the sheep before other visitors happen by to enjoy them.

At the west end of Horseshoe Park, it is easy to see flood damage caused on July 15, 1982, when a dam broke. The Lawn Lake dam predated the establishment of the national park and was built to store irrigation water for use on the plains. This private holding in the national park was not properly maintained, and it deteriorated to the breaking point. In a few minutes it destroyed the cathedral-like beauty of Roaring River, previously one of the most idyllic and easily accessible streams in the park.

Note the thickness of the forest as the road climbs a north-facing slope above Horseshoe Park to meet the beginning of Trail Ridge Road atop Deer Ridge. Trail Ridge Road is one of the world's preeminent scenic highways. The highest continuous paved road in America, Trail Ridge climbs to 12,183 feet above sea level, with 11 miles of the route above tree line. It is closed by wind and snow at least from October through May.

Montane-zone plants blend into subalpine plants amid the beaver ponds of Hidden Valley. The region between 9,000 and 11,500 feet gets the most moisture, averaging 22 inches a year. Most of this comes as snow blown off the alpine tundra above tree line to accumulate in the subalpine zone.

The main trees here are short-needled conifers—the Engelmann spruce and subalpine fir. The most obvious wildlife is seen when you pause at scenic turnouts such as Many Parks Curve and Rainbow Curve. Three members of the jay family are common—the blue Steller's jay, the aptly named gray jay, and Clark's nutcracker with its long bill and snappy black-and-white wings. Representing the rodents are chipmunks with stripes on their faces; golden-mantled ground squirrels, which are bigger and have no stripes on their faces; and red squirrels, which are brown.

Above Rainbow Curve, Trail Ridge Road passes briefly through a ghost forest of limber pines killed by a long-ago fire. Self-portraits sculpted by winter winds that frequently exceed 100 miles per hour, limber pines

survive by bending before the gales and taking shelter behind rocks. Life is tenuous and growth imperceptible where mountain-climbing forests are driven back by the wind and low temperatures.

The wind will not permit any large plants above tree line, where any that dare to stand erect are killed for their impertinence. The survivors on rolling tundra uplands are ground-hugging plants. In a climate where there is no frost-free season and snowstorms are no surprise on any day of the year, most of the flowers wear hairy coats that retard desiccation by the wind and help preserve warmth. All but one of the alpine tundra flowers along Trail Ridge are perennials. It takes more than one very short summer for most tundra plants to grow and reproduce.

Yet this austere land above the trees can be the most delightful of any area in the mountains. Most of its flowers bloom at once, unlike the species at lower altitudes, which have a longer season in which to spread out the flowering. Moreover, tundra blossoms tend to be very large in proportion to the tiny size of the plant. Time in which fertilization can take place is so short that tundra plants cannot afford to be subtle about attracting insects to spread pollen. Like gaudy billboards, their large flowers scream at insects, "Come taste my excellent nectar *right now!* Only a few days left! HURRY! HURRY!"

The largest bloom on the tundra belongs to the alpine sunflower, two to four inches across. This golden disk always faces east, providing a far better compass than moss on tree trunks, particularly in a treeless environment. It may be that an alpine sunflower can produce such large blossoms because it spends years growing a thick taproot and hairy leaves. After this preparation, the sunflower bursts into glorious bloom, attracting many pollinating insects and setting many seeds. Then, exhausted, the plant dies. While very common in any tundra summer, alpine sunflowers in some (unpredictable) summers mass in awesome carpets of yellow.

Driving thousands of plant miles in less than 50 road miles is easiest on well-maintained Trail Ridge Road. But there are many roads in Colorado that pass above tree line. Two others were built strictly for tourism: roads on Pikes Peak and Mount Evans. Both climb over 14,000 feet into the sky.

The highest paved road in the United States scales

Volunteers round up MacGregor Ranch cattle on the edge of Rocky Mountain National Park. Legacy of a family that pioneered Estes Park in 1874, the ranch today operates as an educational foundation, a beautiful and valuable resource for area schools and visitors from across the nation.

Mount Evans, where tree line is delineated by uncommon and ancient bristlecone pines. Some of these gnarled gnomes of tree line are 2,000 years old, and many exceed 1,000 years. Twisted, bent, and battered, they are nonetheless majestic in their successful struggle against time and fierce elements.

The rest of the high-altitude roads were built for utility rather than scenery. Coincidentally, they cross very high passes amid spectacular views. These include paved highways over Independence, Loveland, and Berthoud passes.

Fortunately, the bulk of motorists who travel high-altitude roads rarely venture far from their cars. Destruc-

tion of tundra plants close to roads would be substantial if all high-altitude drivers decided to take a hike. Some wear and tear already is obvious.

Although tundra plants are said to be delicate, they actually are incredibly tough. So harsh is their environment that only very rugged plants stand any chance of survival. However, they are balanced constantly on the edge of death just due to natural hazards. A few stray footsteps or an accidentally lost piece of litter can be all that is needed to tip the balance against life.

Therefore, on heavily visited alpine tundra along roads, care is particularly necessary. Try to step on rocks. Avoid stepping on plants that others have trod

The bighorn sheep is the state animal of Colorado and symbol of Rocky Mountain National Park. A ram's massive horns take seven to eight years to reach full curl and are used for crashing combat.

A mule-deer buck roams among ponderosa pines in the montane zone. Heavy snow forces mule deer off the heights in winter, but in summer they range from the alpine tundra down to the plains. Their large ears, which move separately and nearly constantly, give this species its name.

upon. When a path already exists, stay on it. Picking tundra flowers, or any wildflowers, on public land is against the law in Colorado and subject to a $500 fine.

So popular has hiking become in Rocky Mountain National Park and such national wilderness areas as Indian Peaks, Holy Cross, and Rawah that damage is evident on some alpine tundra remote from roads. The frequently used expression that describes wilderness lovers stomping the wilderness into mud is "loving it to death." The old motto, "Take only pictures, leave only footprints," has been cut in half; now footprints are too much to leave.

Wilderness ethics often are summarized by the admonition to "leave no trace." Axes have no more role in the woods than do cavalry sabers. Digging is done with plastic trowels for the one and only purpose of disposing of human wastes. Those who cut across switchbacks in the trail, which causes erosion, are obviously wilderness novices.

Colorado's mountain wilds provide at least three major benefits. First, the wilds are refuges of untamed nature—animals, flowers, trees, streams, precipices—that stimulate intense personal experiences fully involving mind, senses, and emotions. Colorado mountain wilds have this capacity because the high country is excitingly beautiful in ways both grandiose and subtle. It has a simplicity that captures people and a complexity that challenges them.

Second, Colorado's wilds constitute a symbol, like a flag or a cross. They have a meaning that supersedes their physical existence. Untamed mountains symbolize traits widely considered desirable and also traits that are not represented by the normal human and machine-dominated environment of the cities. These desirable traits include self-reliance, independence, self-restraint, and modesty.

Third, these wildernesses provide a variety of "practical" benefits, no more important than the previous two but somewhat more tangible. These include protection of trees and shrubs, whose shade and roots slowly release snowmelt that otherwise would be lost or require the building of expensive reservoirs. Wilderness recreation is very important to Colorado's tourism industry. And large untamed areas also help to filter various pollutants from the air and water.

The benefits of experiencing mountain wilds are not cut off by winter. Ski touring or cross-country skiing is emotionally a technological adaptation of summer hiking. Skis once were called snowshoes, and the main difference between touring skis and the webbed contrivances we call snowshoes is that touring skis normally are easier to use.

Because you can ski tour whenever the snow is deep enough to cover most of the rocks, opportunities for cross-country skiing in the Colorado Rockies are literally limitless. Groomed trails, although convenient, are not essential to the cross-country skier, for whom snow is a highway into living winter. Wild animals are fewer in number than during lazy summer but easier to see after leaves have fallen. Animals write the adventures of their lives with tracks in the snow. Their ephemeral tales often are long and complex. Wilderness skiers sometimes are very slow in their progress from point to point, constantly delayed by interpreting the runes of wildlife sagas.

Interest in ski touring is booming to gold-rush proportions. All major Colorado ski resorts feature cross-country activities as part of their allure. A few of the most prominent ski-touring centers include Steamboat Springs, home of Swen Wiik, the state's cross-country guru and instructor without peer. The Tenth Mountain Division Trail between Vail and Aspen features a system of huts that can provide shelter for five to seven days of touring through winter wonder. Copper Mountain along Interstate 70 and Purgatory in the awesome San Juan Mountains also offer fine cross-country skiing schools.

Along Colorado Highway 14 near Cameron Pass, 7 Utes Resort is a small ski-touring center that features unusually good snow east of the continental divide. Colorado Mountain Club huts are peppered at strategic spots for ski touring across the state. Devils Thumb Ranch near Fraser is the site of many major cross-country skiing races.

Alpine, or downhill, skiing, while requiring some of the same skills and superficially similar equipment, is quite different from cross-country skiing. Downhill skiing is something else (or, as some adherents would say, "Something ELSE!"). It is exciting. It often is lovely in the same way that a deer jumping over a log is lovely. It

Modern architecture festoons the base of Peak Nine ski slopes at Breckenridge. Some of Colorado's finest resorts are old mining towns that have gained new life by exploiting "white gold."

takes place in areas of extreme, mostly untamed beauty. It promotes self-reliance to the extent that it demands developing an individual's skills. But it is not uncrowded, independent recreation, for ski slopes are expensive operations that demand high use to generate a profit. Downhill skiing is a unique combination of both wilderness and urban experiences.

Many ski resorts have pumped new life into formerly dying mining towns. White gold floating down to the mountain slopes has replaced mineral gold excavated from the mountain cores. Such recycled mining towns include very picturesque Breckenridge, Aspen, and Telluride. Start-from-scratch ski resorts include Vail along Interstate 70 and Silver Creek, recently opened near Granby. One of the most popular ski resorts is Winter Park, developed at the west portal of an engineering wonder, the Moffat Railroad Tunnel under the continental divide, route of weekend ski trains. Copper Mountain, also along Interstate 70, boasts the ideal in skiing terrain: Its beginning, intermediate, and expert slopes all are separate from each other on various sides of the mountain.

For skier or backpacker, motorist or mountaineer, for the multitude who are all of these at one time or another, the lure of the Colorado Rockies is irresistible. The peaks and valleys, forests and snowfields, streams and lakes, flowers and wildlife create a mood, a feeling, a dream that today is the state's most important resource.

Nearly everyone who has experienced Colorado's

Its economy today based on tourism, Breckenridge uses its boomtown heritage as a theme to attract visitors. Horse-drawn taxis haul skiers to shops in restored mining-era buildings on Main Street.

This Lionshead ski lift on Vail Mountain in White River National Forest offers views of the Gore Range in Eagles Nest Wilderness Area.

Rocky Mountain country would agree with one of the first tourists, the English Earl of Dunraven. In 1873, he attempted to establish a wildlife preserve in approximately the area of today's Rocky Mountain National Park. His public relations were inadequate, and he ran afoul of American settlers who wanted pieces of Estes Park for themselves. Dunraven failed to establish his preserve, but he never shook off the allure of high country magic. "Colorado," the Earl later wrote, "is health-giving—unsurpassed, as I believe, anywhere—giving to the jaded spirit, the unstrung nerves, and weakened body, a stimulant, a tone and vigor that can only be appreciated by those who have had the good fortune to travel or reside in that region."

Experiencing the State: Places to Visit in Colorado

ANTONITO (F-4)* is the beginning point for the Cumbres and Toltec Scenic Railroad, a narrow-gauge time machine that carries passengers back into the 1880s.

ARAPAHO NATIONAL FOREST (C-4) sprawls across north central Colorado, encompassing some of the state's most important mining districts. But today, as always, the most significant treasure of Arapaho National Forest is its incalculable wealth of mountain scenery. These vistas reach their spiritual heights in Eagles Nest and Indian Peaks national wilderness areas (the latter partially in Roosevelt National Forest). The most accessible summit is Mount Evans, 14,264 feet above sea level, reached via Colorado Highway 5, the highest auto road in the United States. Crumbling ghost towns, such as Corona on Rollins Pass, contrast with lively, booming ski resorts, such as Winter Park.

ASPEN (D-3), once the world's most productive silver-mining town, now is a very famous ski resort. Outstanding cultural events are staged here in summer. Hikers and backpackers enjoy the outstanding scenery in nearby Maroon Bells–Snowmass Wilderness Area.

BENT'S OLD FORT NATIONAL HISTORIC SITE (E-6) is a very fine reconstruction of one of the most important forts in American history. Built as a fur-trading post in the 1830s, it was a vital element in the Manifest Destiny ambitions that made the United States a continental nation. National Park Service portrayal of daily life at the fort constitutes a superior display of living history.

BLACK CANYON OF THE GUNNISON NATIONAL MONUMENT (D-2) encompasses 12 miles of the deepest, narrowest, most awesome canyon in Colorado. Cut by the Gunnison River, Black Canyon is accessible by car on both rims. Most visitors approach from the south side from near Montrose.

BOULDER (C-4) is the home of the University

of Colorado, whose roofs of red tile on sandstone buildings complement views of the Flatirons, sandstone slabs that tower above the city. Also part of the campus is the Mary Rippon Outdoor Theater, where the Colorado Shakespeare Festival is held each summer. The National Center for Atmospheric Research exemplifies the highly technical scientific study carried on in Boulder and offers visitors exhibits on astronomy, weather, and other atmospheric events.

BRECKENRIDGE (C-4) was born as a gold-mining town in 1859 and named for then Vice-President of the United States John Breckinridge. When Breckinridge deserted the United States for the Confederacy in 1861, the patriotic miners irately changed the spelling of their town's name to dishonor the newly appointed Southern general. Today, however, the citizens of Breckenridge are secessionists themselves, proclaiming the town to be an independent kingdom. Through a cartographic oversight, the town was left out of an official government survey. Feeling unwanted, the residents set up their own country, and signs at the city limits today announce entrance to the Kingdom of Breckenridge. The kingdom has no king but is ruled more or less benevolently by the Norse god of winter, Ull, who creates superb skiing on Breckenridge's complex of slopes. To assure continued abundant snow, Breckenridge devotees of Ull each winter stage an Ullr Fest among the restored Victorian buildings housing shops and restaurants on the charming main street.

CENTRAL CITY (C-4) was Colorado's first and most famous mining boomtown. The original mood is closely duplicated as it booms again for tourists. Each summer, excellent singing reverberates in the acoustically superb Central City Opera House. Tours are available of the restored Teller House and nearby gold mines.

CLIMAX (C-3) at Fremont Pass near Leadville is the site of the largest molybdenum mine in

the world. Since only the very careful and facile of tongue can pronounce the name of this vital metal, it usually is called moly. Used for many purposes, moly finds its main value in the hardening of steel.

COLORADO NATIONAL MONUMENT (D-1) is just barely within the state, a short way off Interstate 70 near Grand Junction. Its maze of desert canyons are most easily viewed from Rim Rock Drive, a 22-mile loop along the rim of thousand-foot-deep canyons decorated by colorful monoliths of fantastically eroded rock.

COLORADO SPRINGS (D-5) has been a popular tourist destination since it was founded for that purpose in 1871. Set at the base of Pikes Peak, the Springs is most famous for its collection of red erosional sculpture in Garden of the Gods and for the 17-spired metal-and-glass architecture of the U.S. Air Force Academy Chapel.

CREEDE (E-3) competed strenuously for the title of toughest mining camp in Colorado. Silver still is mined in Creede, but the wilder forms of recreation have been exchanged for recreation in the wilds of Weminuche and La Garita national wilderness areas and Wheeler Geological Area.

CRESTED BUTTE (D-3) is an old coal-mining town reborn as a ski resort. It also is a gateway to the historic and scenic Ohio Pass and Kebler Pass roads in Gunnison National Forest.

CRIPPLE CREEK (D-4) was the last and richest of Colorado's gold boomtowns. It grew up in the 1890s on the back side of Pikes Peak and serves mainly as a tourist destination today. Higher gold prices recently have caused a resurgence in mining.

CURECANTI NATIONAL RECREATION AREA (E-2) contains three reservoirs—Blue Mesa, Morrow Point, and Crystal—that are

*Letter and number refer to coordinates on map of Colorado, pp. 6-7.

part of the Colorado River Storage Project. Most activity centers on 20-mile-long Blue Mesa.

DENVER (C-5) is Colorado's capital, a mile high in elevation at the capitol building steps. Financial center for the entire Rocky Mountain region, Denver is a booming city, with new glass towers added constantly to the skyline. It boasts fine museums, a topflight zoo, and fascinating botanic gardens. These combine with the restored old Denver shopping area of Larimer Square and the Denver Center for the Performing Arts to make Colorado's capital a fun and fascinating city.

DINOSAUR NATIONAL MONUMENT (B-1) in the northwest corner of Colorado extends into Utah. In fact, the quarry of dinosaur fossils that the monument originally was established to preserve is across the state line. But the bulk of the monument's magnificent canyon scenery is in Colorado, a wilderness maze cut by the Yampa and Green rivers.

FAIRPLAY (D-4) was founded in South Park by miners disgruntled with the treatment they had received from early claimants to mines in nearby Tarryall. Fair play evidently was the best policy, because Fairplay surpassed Tarryall and survives today on tourism. South Park City is a collection of old buildings salvaged from all over South Park and assembled in Fairplay to portray a nineteenth-century mining town.

FLORISSANT FOSSIL BEDS NATIONAL MONUMENT (D-4), west of Colorado Springs, preserves 6,000 acres of the world's most extensive deposits of insect and leaf fossils, delicately turned to stone within the ash of volcanic eruptions 34 to 35 million years ago. A visitor center in an old ranch building displays many local fossils. Along a nature trail are stone stumps of massive redwoods, which millions of years ago thrived far beyond their modern California range.

The monument's name is from a French word meaning "flowering." National Park Service rangers frequently must explain to visitors who confuse *florissant* and *fluorescent* that the fossils do not glow in the dark. But meadows of Indian paintbrush, loco, lupine, and other wildflowers do glow with abundant color in the daytime. With second-home development booming around the monument's borders, it may be

that the preservation of some flowery fields is even more meaningful than the preservation of long-dead plants.

FORT GARLAND (F-4) now is a farming community in the San Luis Valley. But in 1858 the fort for which the town was named protected the region from Indian raids. Colonel Kit Carson commanded the post in 1866–67. It was abandoned by the army in 1883. Adobe Fort Garland State Historical Monument has been restored to its Carson-era appearance by the State Historical Society of Colorado.

GEORGETOWN (C-4) escaped ghost-town status to become the most picturesque of Colorado's old mining towns. Restoration of Victorian homes to their bonanza-period appearance has made the town a popular and worthwhile attraction along Interstate 70.

GLENWOOD SPRINGS (C-2) boasts the largest outdoor mineral hot springs pool in the world, flowing at a rate of about 2,430 gallons per minute. The pool, which stretches out for 405 feet near the mouth of dramatic Glenwood Canyon, is used year-round. This has been a world-famous spa since the 1890s and remains just as popular today.

GRAND LAKE (B-4) is 12 miles long and a mile wide, formed by glaciers thousands of years ago, the largest natural lake in Colorado. The village of Grand Lake boasts the highest yacht harbor in the world (8,135 feet). It also is the gateway community to the west side of Rocky Mountain National Park.

Grand Lake is the smallest of a complex of lakes (the others are dammed reservoirs) that is part of the Colorado–Big Thompson Project, also known as Big T. This massive diversion moves water from the moist western side of the continental divide to the arid eastern slope. As part of the political give-and-take that went into creating Big T, Grand Lake was guaranteed permanent fullness. But the reservoir levels fluctuate drastically in the manner of their kind, responding to water needs on the eastern slope. The reservoirs are contained in Arapaho National Recreation Area.

GREAT SAND DUNES NATIONAL MONUMENT (E-4) testifies that the wide, flat, arid San Luis Valley is a windy place. Three passes funnel winds across a windbreak formed by a massive ridge of 14,345-foot-high Blanca

Peak. As the winds rise over the ridge, they drop grains of sand that they have carried from the valley, a scantily vegetated desert. Over the last 15,000 years, 50 square miles of sand have accumulated in this sheltered spot at the base of the Sangre de Cristo Mountains. These highest inland sand dunes in the United States are constantly reshaped by the wind, some dunes rising as high as 700 feet above the valley floor.

HOVENWEEP NATIONAL MONUMENT (F-1) is a collection of six Anasazi Indian sites, four in Colorado and two in Utah. Constructed by the same culture that built Mesa Verde's cliff dwellings, Hovenweep is much less visited than its famous cousin. Access is by unpaved roads from McElmo, Colorado, and Bluff, Utah. During rainy weather, check locally about the condition of these roads, which may be temporarily impassable.

INDIAN PEAKS WILDERNESS (C-4) borders Rocky Mountain National Park on the south in Roosevelt and Arapaho national forests. Indian Peaks is very easy to reach from Brainard Lake, near the old mining town of Ward, as well as from several other points on both sides of the continental divide. Its scenery and wildflowers are second to none in the state. Therefore, like the national park, Indian Peaks is jammed with hikers, who need to take special care to walk gently on the land. Uninformed hikers who return to their cars with bouquets of freshly picked and already wilting wildflowers are lucky if abundant and zealous wilderness protectors deliver only verbal assaults.

LEADVILLE (C-3) is the highest incorporated community in the United States, about 10,200 feet above sea level. Incredibly rich silver mines created Leadville on the upper reaches of the Arkansas River in the late 1870s. Various restored buildings and museums tell the fabulous story of the still-active mining town, and a nine-mile "Silver Kings Highway" wanders past formerly rich diggings.

MESA VERDE NATIONAL PARK (F-1) was established in 1906, one of the foremost archaeological sites in the world. Mesa Verde is Spanish for "green table," and its cliff dwellings create a magical place, suspended 2,000 feet above the Mancos River Valley. Twenty-one miles of twisting mountain road separate the ruins from the outside world.

MONTE VISTA and **ALAMOSA NATIONAL WILDLIFE REFUGES** (F-4), near the towns for which they are named, are not particularly outstanding for their scenery unless you happen to be a sandhill crane. If so, the refuges are beautiful indeed, and thousands of these huge birds drop in here to rest during their spring and fall migrations between Idaho and New Mexico.

Scattered among the sandhills are a few whooping cranes, among the rarest of North American birds and symbol of all endangered species. The U.S. Fish and Wildlife Service removes spare eggs from whooping-crane nests in Wood Buffalo National Park in Canada and places them in sandhill-crane nests at Grays Lake National Wildlife Refuge in Idaho. The eggs then are hatched by the sandhills, who act as foster parents. The whoopers then adopt the sandhills' migratory habits. The goal is to get a second whooper flock started to help shield the species from the extinction that might occur if the one small natural flock, which winters along the Texas coast, should be wiped out in a single huge disaster.

Picking out the few whoopers from among thousands of widely scattered sandhills has the potential for creating a proverb about frustration. However, whoopers are bigger than sandhills and conspicuous by their partially white color in fall and nearly pure white in spring.

OURAY (E-2) is named for a peace-loving Ute chief and is built on land formerly roamed by the Utes. The jagged mountains rising steeply above Ouray convey to the town the title "Switzerland of America." Scenic Ouray also claims to be the "jeeping capital of the United States" because so many old mining roads cling to the cliffs of the surrounding San Juan Mountains and are suitable only for four-wheel-drive vehicles.

PIKES PEAK (D-4) towers above the high plains of Colorado as a monument to the power of alliteration. Its name is very easy to remember, and it has symbolized Colorado since the Pike exploration reported home in 1807. At 14,110 feet, it is thought by many to be the state's tallest peak, but in fact more than thirty of the state's fifty-plus 14,000-foot mountains are higher. Neither is it particularly striking in appearance compared with Fourteeners like Longs Peak, Mount of the Holy Cross, or the Maroon Bells.

On the other hand, if the mountain itself does not rate among the finest views in Colorado, the view from the top may be in the running. There are at least two hiking trails to the top. But most of the 250,000 folks who yearly reach the summit do so by cog railway from Manitou Springs or by the automobile toll road. For drivers affected by altitude sickness or who are disinclined to face the road on the trip down, there are chauffeurs for hire at the gift shop on top.

ROCKY MOUNTAIN NATIONAL PARK (B-4) is said to be the state's most popular attraction. Its mountains, crowned by 14,255-foot Longs Peak, are as spectacular as any in the state and considerably more accessible than most. Most of the park's summer visitors drive up Trail Ridge Road, which climbs 5,000 feet on its 44-mile course and then drops 4,000 feet on the way to Grand Lake at the west entrance.

Open all year is a very popular nine-mile spur road to Bear Lake, dominated by the sheer face of Hallett Peak (12,713 feet). Bear Lake also is the most used of the trailheads in the national park, which contains more than 350 miles of trail. Sheer rock walls, like the face of Hallett Peak, draw many climbers to this park. National Park Service rescue teams get a lot of practice and are very proficient.

For history-minded visitors, the national park contains two interesting old ranches. Never Summer Ranch is a park service living-history demonstration of early-twentieth-century dude ranching, on the west side of the park. MacGregor Ranch, on the outskirts of the gateway community of Estes Park Village, is a foundation-owned holding which preserves the cattle ranching that began here a century ago.

ROYAL GORGE (D-4) is a Canon City park. From the world's highest suspension bridge across the canyon, its sheer walls drop 1,055 feet to the Arkansas River. An aerial tramway also spans the gorge, and an incline railway descends to the bottom. A good, free view of the canyon can be had from a picnic ground reached via a .7-mile side road that leaves the main road just less than a mile inside the park entrance. Early morning is the best time for photos.

Perhaps an even more famous landmark of Canon City is the Colorado State Prison. The favorite town legend maintains that the community chose to host the prison rather than a state university, believing that the former would likely attract a larger enrollment.

SILVERTON (E-2) supposedly was named in the 1870s because the surrounding mines had "silver by the ton." Mining still goes on, but tourism also is an important source of income. The colorful old mining town set amid the spectacular volcanic peaks of the San Juans is a terminus of a narrow-gauge railroad, called the Silverton, that makes a very popular run from Durango.

STEAMBOAT SPRINGS (B-3) began as a supply center for surrounding ranches in the Yampa Valley. But today it thrives on winter sports. The waters from some of the area's approximately 150 springs feed pools where sore and weary skiers can relax. The summer beauty of surrounding Routt National Forest makes Steamboat a recreation center also during the June through September months of mediocre skiing.

TELLURIDE (E-2) is another mining town recycled as a ski resort. Through good sense and hard work, it has preserved many of its Victorian mining-town buildings. But modern ski architecture also is to be found in the amphitheater of astounding mountains that surround Telluride and the headwaters of the San Miguel River. Nearby ghost towns, such as Alta, demonstrate how other mining camps fared without the development of ski slopes.

VAIL (C-3) is one of the few ski towns in Colorado that did not begin as a mining town. Rather, it is a planned community designed by World War II mountain troops who had trained at nearby Camp Hale and recognized the area's near-perfect snow conditions. Jammed into a narrow valley with Interstate 70, Vail is the portal to the largest one-mountain ski area in North America. Other slopes are nearby.

Although summer is off-season in Vail, this imitation Tyrolean community offers much during "poor skiing season," the locals' synonym for summer. For instance, a gondola ski lift hoists summer hikers to high-altitude trails with fine views of Eagles Nest and Holy Cross wilderness areas in White River National Forest. Also available to visitors at all times of the year are the Vail Nature Center and the Colorado Ski Museum.